RIPTIDES By Robert O'Brien

He makes maps. He lives in a room on the fourth floor of the Montgomery Block, and I would say he's in his thirties. His name is Ken Cathcart.

He makes these maps and sells them for a living. And while he doesn't seem to be broke, he doesn't exactly seem to be wallowing in cash, either. The maps would look high priced to the average purse, and I guess they are. But when you put a lot of work into something, you're certainly entitled to ask what you think it's worth. Maybe you don't make a million, but anyway, you're not selling yourself short.

There are three different maps, and two more that are in preparation. He calls the three: "Sketch Map of California Gold Region, with Notes and Memorabilia Chiefly of the Golden Era;" "A Map of San Francisco Bay Region," and "A Map of Old San Francisco, Circa 1854, Showing the Heart of the Town, with Historical Notes and Memorabilia for the Lusty Years of a Century."

The two on their way up are things in the same spirit on Chinatown and the city as mapped in the early-day history, "Annals of San Francisco."

The way he does them is to draw the map, border it elaborately, put in hundreds of tiny, but appropriate illustrative drawings, reproduce it by a photographic process and then tint it by hand with ink or water colors. To give you an idea of how they're loaded with detail, there are nearly 50 ships shown on the water areas of the Bay Region map (its overall measurements are 14 by 14 inches). They all have some connection with the history of the port, and range from Drake's Golden Hind to the battlewagon

South Dakota, which came in with Admiral Halsey and the Third Fleet in 1945.

Cathcart, who was born in Kansas and landed in San Francisco 10 or 11 years ago by way of Denver and Seattle, got mixed up with maps in a rather oblique sort of way. He put together a book on Chinatown, which failed to click with the publishers, and started to gather material for a book on the Montgomery Block. In the process of research, he found that a good way to keep track of information like the locations of old buildings was to make maps which plainly showed where their sites had been. So when the Chinatown book didn't go over, and as his map notes for the Montgomery Block book grew, he put them together and started the work he's now doing.

"Rather than be a frustrated author, I'm producing something," is his way of putting it. "And, anyway, a map is like a book, a one-page book. You could write a thousand stories on the material in the old San Francisco map."

He kept repeating that one of his main interests was to explode the numerous myths that blur the facts of San Francisco life.

"I'm all for debunking the phony legends about the town," he said. "They ought to be stabbed whenever you get the chance."

For instance:

"Well, they say Jack London used to live in this block. I can't find any truth to that. I don't think George Sterling lived here, either. There was a room here that was available to him, when he wanted it, but I can't find anything that says he ever resided here.

"Then, they say this building is built on redwood mats. It is in front, but it isn't in back. I know,

because I've taken photographs of the pilings.

"And there's Pisco punch. There wasn't anything mysterious about it. It was made of pineapple juice —a delicacy from the Sandwich islands in those days—and a Peruvian brandy. I got that from Duncan Nicol's old bartender."

Cathcart also takes sides in the controversy about the date of the naming of San Francisco. One group of supporters says the proclamation was issued January 23, 1847, but wasn't published until the January 30 issue of the California Star; therefore the 30th was the day the city officially stopped being Yerba Buena, and became San Francisco. Cathcart believes the proclamation was issued and published on the 23rd, and that any one who says the anniversary is January 30 is a week off.

There's also the fable about Jenny Lind, who never sang here, in spite of the old timers who have sworn they heard her sing from a San Francisco stage. Cathcart turned up another about Emperor Norton, who some authorities say lived on Sacramento street. "Maybe they're wrong, but the old city directories say he lived at 624 Commercial street. He paid his landlady 50 cents a day for his room—probably the only cash transaction he made as Emperor Norton."

Sometimes you can't even trust the old, official record. Duplicating them, for instance, Cathcart's San Francisco map spells Kearny street "Kearney," and Sansome street "Sansom." Aside from that, they looked fine to me.

And aside from that, the old timer who approaches the maps with the idea of tearing them apart for their inaccuracies, had better watch it, or he'll end up buying them.

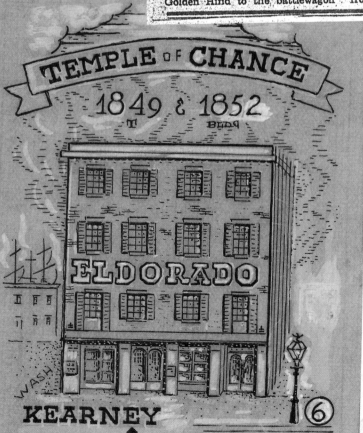

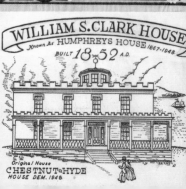

GOLD MOUNTAIN
BIG CITY

Ken Cathcart's 1947 Illustrated Map
of San Francisco's Chinatown

Written by JIM SCHEIN

Foreword by GORDON CHIN

Designed by IAIN R. MORRIS

CAMERON + COMPANY
Petaluma, California

Guide to the interesting places in
S. F. CHINATOWN

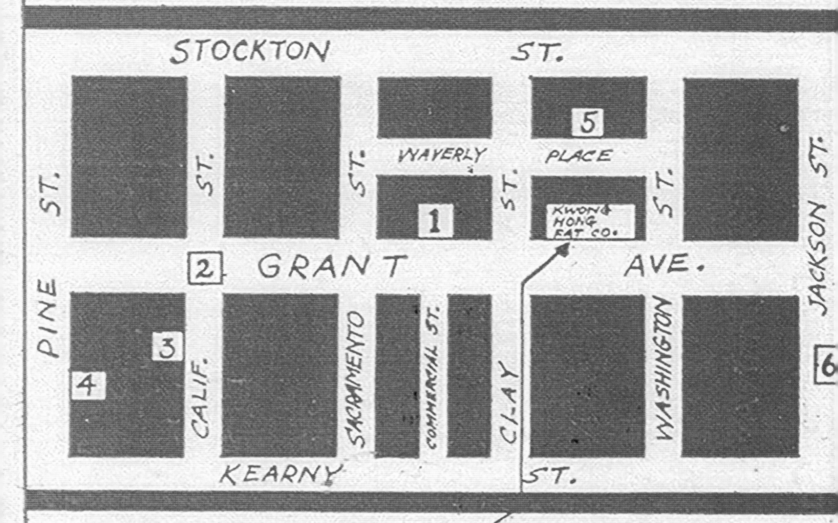

KWONG HONG FAT CO.
837 GRANT AVENUE

1. BUDDHA FINE ARTS
717 GRANT AVE.

2. CABLE CARS
CALIF. & GRANT

3. DR. SUN YET SEN'S MEMERIAL
CALIF. & PINE

4. KONG CHOW TEMPLE
520 PINE ST.

5. TIN HOW TEMPLE
125 WAVERLY PL.

6. CHINESE OPERA THEATER
636 JACKSON ST.

TABLE OF CONTENTS

ENDPAPERS: *This 1947 San Francisco* Chronicle *article on Ken Cathcart by Robert O'Brien provides a rare interview with the mapmaker. The background images are sketches that Cathcart created to support the stories in his seven maps.*
PAGE 1: *Grant Avenue at night, looking north (Cathcart, 1938).*
PAGES 2–3: *Looking north toward the Chinatown tennis courts; tennis was very popular in the '30s and '40s in Chinatown (Cathcart, 1938).*
OPPOSITE: *Business card map of the mid-twentieth century; merchants promoted important Chinatown sites and their locations.*

FOREWORD

BY GORDON CHIN

SINCE JIMMIE AND MARTI SCHEIN opened Schein & Schein Old Maps in 2003, Jimmie and I often shared stories about San Francisco, stories about our city's history, diversity, progressive politics, and creativity. Before I retired in 2011, I headed the Chinatown Community Development Center just down the street from Schein & Schein, on Upper Grant Avenue. I loved checking out the latest maps, photos, and artifacts in their window.

A couple of years ago, Jimmie told me about the Ken Cathcart Chinatown historic photo collection on the Schein & Schein website. It is an amazing collection, with over a thousand images of Chinatown from 1936 to 1946, and Jimmie let me use some of the photos for a video my organization was producing about the history of the Chinese Playground.

Jimmie and Marti had acquired the entire Cathcart collection in 2003—over three thousand photos, hundreds of papers, and a number of old maps. At the time, they weren't really sure what they had or even who Ken Cathcart was.

Ken Cathcart was born in Harper, Kansas, in 1902. He came to San Francisco in 1937, a place where he lived a bohemian lifestyle with fellow artists on Montgomery Street before the Beat era. He became fascinated with San Francisco's Chinatown, one of the many segregated sectors of northeast San Francisco. Chinatown was a place that held a special sense of mystique for Euro-American photographers like Arnold Genthe at the turn of the twentieth century, and for Ken Cathcart in the pre- and post-WWII era. While I was familiar with Cathcart's Chinatown photo collection, I didn't know anything about his mapmaking until Jimmie asked me to write the foreword for this book.

San Francisco Chinatown & Environs: A Scrapbook Map is the title of Cathcart's 1947 map about Chinatown. It is an illustrated map, a popular map genre in those days, which some called "cartoon maps." The colorful map includes 151 icons of important scenes and places in Chinatown of that time, and twenty-six vignettes, images of Chinese American history since the earliest Chinese emigration in the mid-nineteenth century, from Sun Yat-sen to Chinese railroad workers who built the Transcontinental Railroad. The 1947 map is a fascinating historical artifact, which Jimmie Schein has meticulously researched and beautifully displayed.

In *Gold Mountain, Big City: Ken Cathcart's 1947 Illustrated Map of San Francisco's Chinatown*, Schein gives a brief overview of other Chinatown maps over the last century, starting with the infamous 1885 map produced for the federal government after the passage of the 1882 Chinese Exclusion Act, marking the first time in American history that any racial group was excluded by virtue of their race. This map depicted Chinatown's land use, not only the usual elements found in city planning maps (residential uses, parks, major institutions, manufacturing, etc.) but also opium dens, gambling houses, and places of both Chinese and white prostitution. As such, the 1885 map was very prominently used as a justification for Chinese exclusion.

Cathcart's 1947 map was, in part, an attempt to create a more positive image of Chinatown. The Chinatown of the 1880s was destroyed in the 1906 San Francisco earthquake and fire, and the new Chinatown was rebuilt with ornate, stylized Chinese pagoda-topped buildings, a strategy to thwart efforts from San Francisco business leaders to relocate Chinatown and take over its land. While the newly rebuilt Chinatown (without the gambling, opium, or prostitution dens) was not forced out of its original neighborhood, Chinese Americans continued to suffer from racism and discrimination. It was Chinese American support of the WWII effort that presented the opportunity to enhance the Chinese community's image and political clout in the postwar era.

With the support of Chinatown friends such as B.S. Fong, the Chinese Six Companies commissioned Ken Cathcart to design a new Chinatown map, one targeted to Western eyes and opinion makers. And while the map does take some creative liberties—inaccuracies in Chinese costume styles, nonsensical Chinese characters on some storefront signs, etc.— the images presented show a Chinatown with vibrant arts and culture, strong leaders and institutions, and one of San Francisco's most unique neighborhoods.

I find it amazing that many of the notable places in the 1947 map had been important Chinatown places for nearly a century—the Chinese Six Companies (1848), Cameron House (1874), and the Chinese Hospital (1924), to name but a few—a testament to the resilience of Chinatown and its leaders to preserve and protect San Francisco's oldest and most historically intact neighborhood.

In her wonderful book of maps *Infinite City: A San Francisco Atlas*, San Francisco author Rebecca Solnit said, "Every place deserves an atlas, an atlas is at least implicit in every place, and to say that is to ask first of all what a place is." Jimmie Schein's book *Gold Mountain, Big City* is one such atlas about San Francisco's Chinatown.

RIGHT: *In this discreet self-portrait, Cathcart captures his reflection and that of his date in an ice-cream parlor mirror (Cathcart, 1938).*

PREFACE

BY JIM SCHEIN

SAN FRANCISCO IS A MAGICAL CITY that has long attracted immigrants, artists, and visionaries from around the world, packing them into its meager forty-nine square miles. Many, like Ken Cathcart, allured by the beauty of the sparkling city by the bay, decide to stay, contributing to its cultural diversity and ensuring that the city remains a primary destination for bohemians and original thinkers.

When I moved to San Francisco as a teenager in 1980, I would frequently run into the landlord of our three-flat building as I headed to work at Butterfield & Butterfield on my skateboard. His question was always, "Did ya read Herb Caen this morning?" I quickly learned that loving San Francisco required dedication to Herb Caen's daily columns, as well as the musings of other notable local writers of that period, such as Carl Nolte and Ben Fong-Torres. Their love affair with San Francisco illustrated and illuminated the traditions and unique character of San Francisco's past, leading me down a path of appreciation, investigation, and investment that I pursued for the next twenty-five years. While living here in North Beach and traveling abroad, I have continually collected maps, stories, and views of San Francisco, the city that I truly love.

It made sense, after retiring from a career in operations for the entertainment business, that my attention turned to the pursuit of San Francisco history. In 2003, my wife, Marti Schein, and I opened Schein & Schein Old Maps in North Beach.

This book starts with the community and the neighborhood where we found an amazing treasure trove of maps, along with a photographic archive of local history. The impressive depth and content of this world-class collection is the result of the determined work of a few people. It was their good judgment, hard work, serious research, and love for one another and for San Francisco that motivated us to continue the project they began.

Artist Kenneth Cathcart's love for San Francisco would not have been discovered if not for the serendipitous connection with our eccentric neighbor, Laura Dorenzo. In 2003, Laura walked into our newly opened shop and told us that she had lots of "maps and stuff" in her basement that we should buy from her. The majority of Laura's collection was from a neighbor whom she had befriended and who had passed away twenty years earlier.

Laura was about eighty years old when we met her. She had been a flight attendant for Flying Tigers airlines, during the heyday of air travel. Laura had traveled the world and saved nearly everything. As we went through her extensive collection—the boxes inside boxes and numerous tubes containing maps and documents—we found many loose maps, along with dusty stacks of things we thought might contain gems. Eventually, we discovered original material by Ken Cathcart. Laura explained that she met him on Telegraph Hill in

BELOW: Flying Tigers was a premier cargo and passenger charter airline, descended from the famed air squadron of the same name that fought the Japanese on behalf of and with the Chinese, before American formal involvement in World War II. Sold in the 1970s, they are now known as FedEx.

OPPOSITE: Sing Chong and Sing Fat, on Grant at California Street, were considered the entryway to Chinatown before World War II.

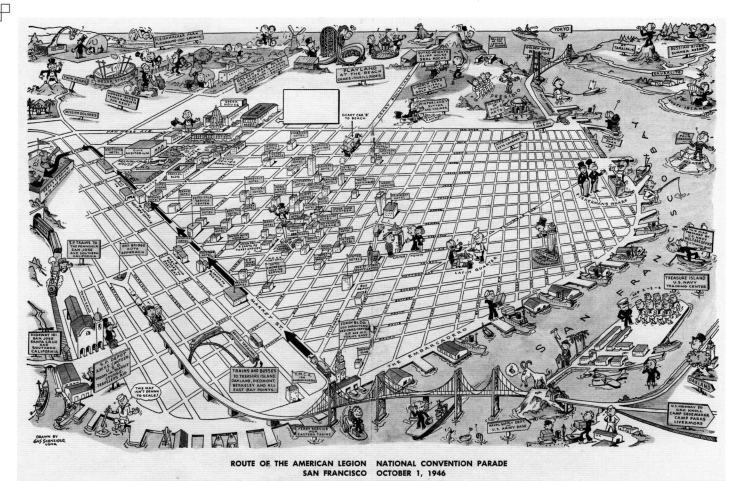

ROUTE OF THE AMERICAN LEGION   NATIONAL CONVENTION PARADE
SAN FRANCISCO   OCTOBER 1, 1946

OPPOSITE, TOP
TO BOTTOM: Gus
Schneider's 1946 map
was made to show
the American Legion
parade route but was
later used to direct
members to the first
UN meetings at the
Civic Center War
Memorial. • Ruth
Taylor White produced
this map in 1939 for
the Mark Hopkins
Hotel, but it was also
used for the Fairmont
across the street and
for the 1939 Golden
Gate International
Exposition (GGIE).

the '60s and that over the next twenty-five years they became very good friends. When he passed away in 1985, his landlord called her, saying "Ken's dead. His relatives don't want anything, and it's all going to the dump tomorrow morning. Stop by and take what you want." Laura took what she thought was relevant: a collection of historic reference maps, manuscript maps, photolithographic plates, and illustrations.

Cathcart had a large collection of more than seventy-five maps: Daniel P. Wallingford's *New Yorkers' Perspective of the United States*, all of Ernest Dudley Chase's maps, and some from Gus Schneider, George Avery, Jo Mora, and Ruth Taylor White. He also had maps of most states and metropolitan areas, including important events for California, Arizona, and New Mexico; major metropolitan cities like San Francisco, New York, and Chicago; and centennial state maps for Oregon, Texas, and California.

As the most prevalent in his collection were twentieth-century illustrated maps, we determined that Cathcart was a focused student and Laura an enthusiast and collector. Often called "cartoon" or "pictorial maps," this genre was most likely started in 1914 by MacDonald Gill and initiated in the United States in 1919 by Ruth Taylor White. It carried on from the 1930s to the 1960s through regional maps created by commercial artists for the open market. Ken Cathcart's calling was to make illustrated maps, and the maps we bought not made by others turned out to be made by him—seven illustrated maps altogether, registered with the Library of Congress and published under his company name, Historic Maps by Ken Cathcart.

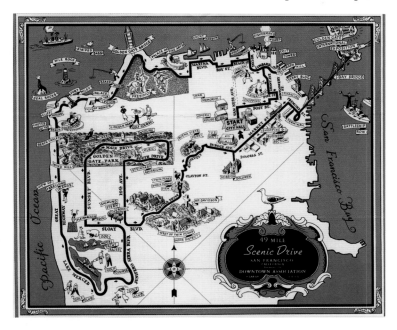

About a year after the initial purchase, Laura came back to the shop with a black wooden box, covered in fabric and loaded with aluminum film vials. Handing it to me, she said, "This is yours. It's Cathcart's photographs." When I asked her what I owed her, she said, "It is part of the deal; you already bought it. Good luck, kid." Laura passed away a couple months later.

ABOVE: The popular
49 Mile Scenic Drive
map of 1939 was
the creation of the
Downtown Merchants
Association to promote
a scenic route to the
fair, with stops at all of
San Francisco's finest
sites along the way.
The journey started at
City Hall and ended
at the GGIE on the
newly built Treasure
Island in the middle of
the Bay.

That box contained Cathcart's entire body of photographic works, from 1930 to 1958, many of which have been included in the first section of this book. While the photos were originally intended for his mapmaking, they became our single best resource for learning about Cathcart and understanding his relationships with San Francisco and the people he met through his work.

When we bought Laura's entire collection, we had no idea what we had in terms of its historical importance. The acquisition did, however, kick-start a decade-long research and photographic project, which led to the publication of this book. We owe a great debt to Laura for introducing us to Ken Cathcart, and to the photographer, artist, and mapmaker whose breadth and depth of work we uncover within these pages.

INTRODUCTION

A MAPMAKER'S LOVE AFFAIR WITH SAN FRANCISCO

KEN CATHCART'S 1947 MAP OF CHINATOWN, *San Francisco's Chinatown and Environs,* paints a surprisingly detailed picture of life in San Francisco's Chinatown in the mid-twentieth century. Some of the map's stories are darker than others, and some reveal an unintended bias reflective of Cathcart's time. The celebratory intent and attempt at historical accuracy is present in all of Cathcart's maps and conveys a desire to be truthful and respectful of race and ethnic origins. The same is said for us, and we find in our research that there are discrepancies in dates, places, or origins due to politics, misspellings, and phonetic translations that depend on whom you ask for a meaning. Modern viewers should approach his work with this mind-set, tempering their own biases and embracing tolerance for his expressive map, which was created more than seventy years ago. Additionally, we ask readers to let us know if they have any corrections or relevant details or facts that may have been omitted.

BELOW: *This is the infamous 1885 Official Map of Chinatown in San Francisco by the special committee of the Board of Supervisors. It was the first to color a ghetto, defining function or use of property, and in this case, inferred immorality. Note that many corner lots within Chinatown were excluded from Chinese ownership or use and are white-owned.*

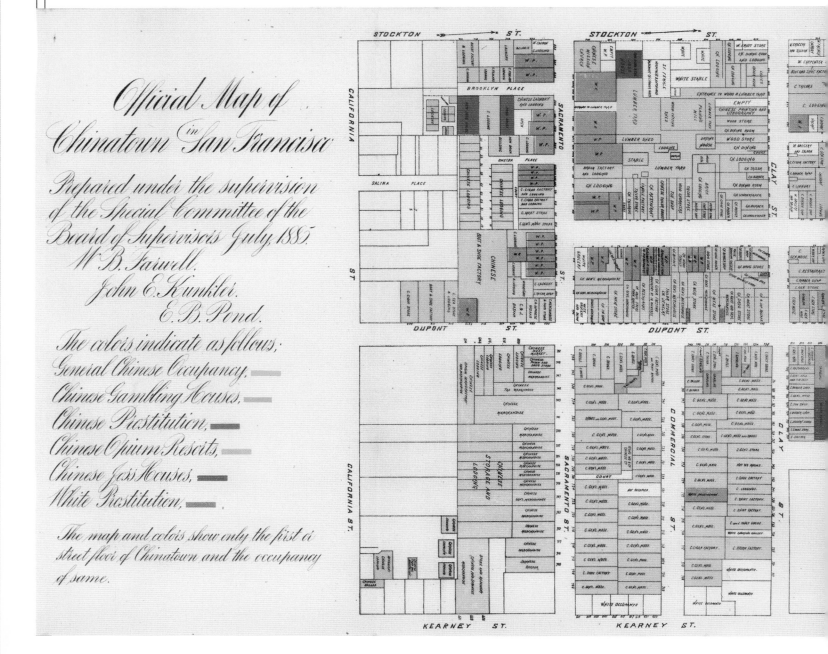

FOLLOWING PAGES:
San Francisco's
Chinatown and
Environs *(1947),
by Kenneth Gwin
Cathcart, was the
fifth of seven maps
produced in his
lifetime and the one
this book explores
in depth. The issue
shown here is a
colored version of the
original brown-and-
tan artist's proof.*

The map is dated, stylized, and "of the period"; it is also well researched and comprehensive. Cathcart combined literal and visual materials to suggest an interpretation that included philosophical, racial, and/or cultural bias, often including humorous—albeit derogatory, stereotypical, or superficial—representation, with tongue firmly planted in cheek. There was a sense of legitimacy in the creation of this map because it fulfilled the same goal of formal maps from earlier periods: to promote San Francisco. This goal hasn't changed in the history of Bay Area mapmaking. These defining features are what unify all seven Cathcart maps and what makes the man who made them so intriguing.

While residing on Telegraph Hill, Cathcart was in close proximity to locals well versed in the history of the area and greater San Francisco. Since there may be no person alive today who knew him, the ideas presented here are extrapolations and are, therefore, hypothetical. Although the information, details, and data provided have created a good and plausible timeline, it is important to note that Cathcart's perspective was not that of a trained historian, mapmaker, or even an author. Rather, it was framed by the goals of documenting and promoting. His research focused on the then-modern idea of updating the marketing of Chinatown history to white locals and tourists.

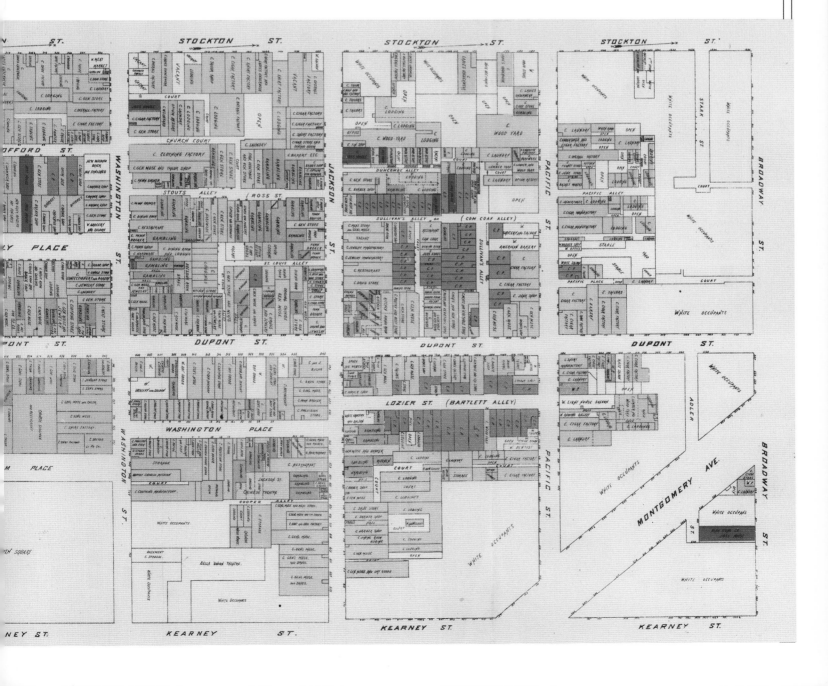

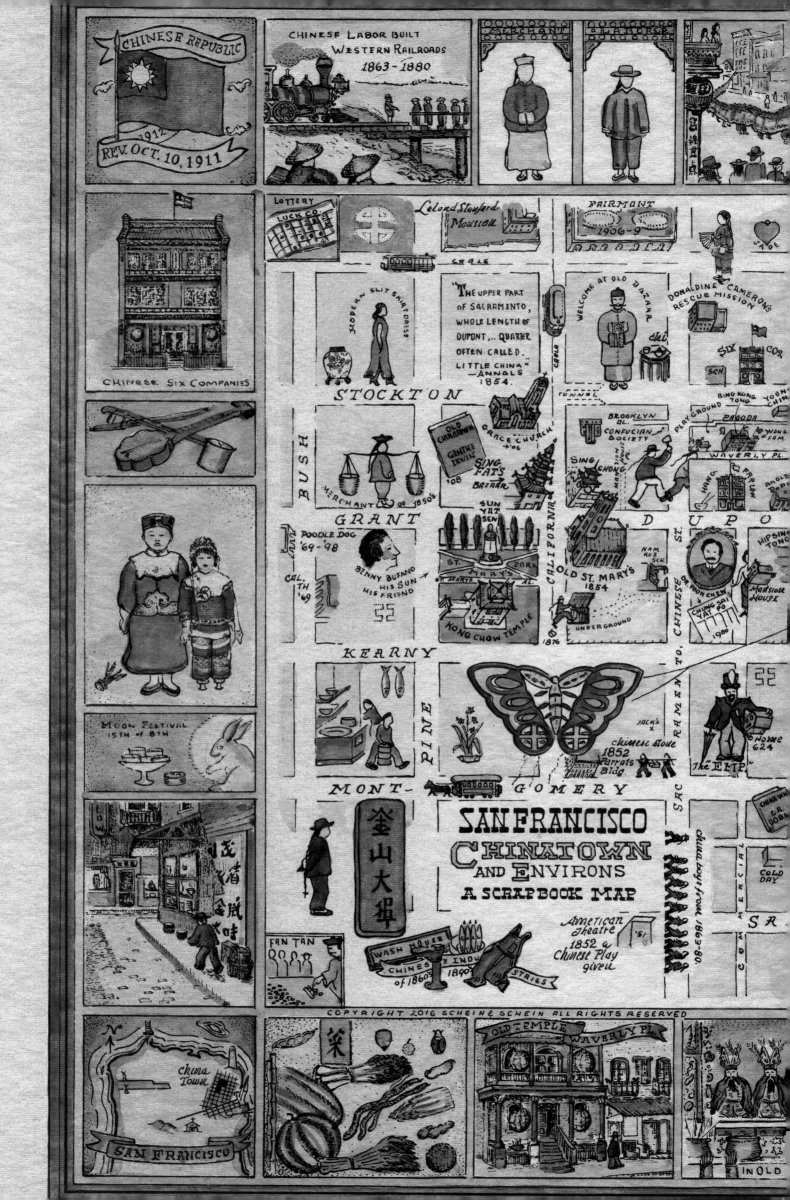

SAN FRANCISCO CHINATOWN AND ENVIRONS
A SCRAPBOOK MAP

CHINESE REPUBLIC
1912
REV. OCT. 10, 1911

CHINESE LABOR BUILT WESTERN RAILROADS 1863-1880

MERCHANT · LABORER

CHINESE SIX COMPANIES

MOON FESTIVAL 15TH OF 8TH

SAN FRANCISCO

China Town

LOTTERY LUCK CO.

Leland Stanford Mansion

FAIRMONT 1906-9

JADE

CABLE

STOCKTON

BUSH

"THE upper part of SACRAMENTO, WHOLE LENGTH of DUPONT,.. QUARTER OFTEN CALLED. LITTLE CHINA" — ANNALS 1854.

MODERN SLIT SKIRT DRESS

WELCOME AT OLD BAZAAR

DONALDINA CAMERON'S RESCUE MISSION

SIX COS.

SCH

GRANT

MERCHANT of 1850's

OLD CHINATOWN GENTHE IRVIN '08

GRACE CHURCH '06

SING FAT'S BAZAAR

SUN YAT SEN

TUNNEL

BROOKLYN AL.

CONFUCIAN SOCIETY

SING CHONG

PLAYGROUND

BING KONG TONG

YOUNG CHINA

PAGODA

WONG FAM.

WAVERLY PL.

HANG FAR LOW

ARNOLD

POODLE DOG '69-98

BENNY BUFANO HIS SUN HIS FRIEND

CAL. TH '69

ST. MARY'S

CORN ST. MARY'S AL.

CALIFORNIA

OLD ST. MARY'S 1854

NAM KUE SCH.

DR. POON CHEW

CHUNG SAI YAT PO 1900

HIP SING TONG

MANSION HOUSE

KEARNY

KONG CHOW TEMPLE

UNDERGROUND 1876

D U P O

PINE

JACK'S Chinese stove 1852 Parrots Bldg

SACRAMENTO, CHINESE ST.

Home 624

The "EMP"

MONT-GOMERY

釜山大埠

FAN TAN

WASH HOUSE CHINESE INDUSTRIES of 1860 & 1890

American Theatre 1852 & Chinese Play given

China boys from 1861-80

COMMERCIAL

COLD DAY

SR

OLD TEMPLE WAVERLY PL.

IN OLD

FARMER — SCHOLAR

LURE of GOLD
1849

MANCHU EMPIRE
1644-1912 A.D.

TELEPHONE EXCHANGE

MAH JONGG

POWELL

TRAY MAN

CON. STOCKTON

CHINESE HOSP.

SCH.

FORTY-NINERS

LONG CHONG or LITTLE PETE DUKE of VICE

CHINESE DIGEST

CHING WAH LEE

1924

SLAVE GIRL

LITTLE MEXICO

TIN HOW TEMPLE HOP SING

CAMERON ALLEY

PAWN SHOP ROSS (STOUT'S) ALLEY of THE GAMBLERS

CHAN FUM

PONTIAC DUMB COMBE

(SULLIVAN) AL.

HOW WONG TEMPLE

PIPE of DREAMS

1st. CHI LAUNDRY

ST. LOUIS AL.

LOOK OUT

BROADWAY

OLD BULLETIN BOARD

SUEY SING TONG

MANDARIN TH.

FUN for HOODLUMS

SALVATION ARMY

TEL. BLDG.

FAMILIES (WASH AL.)

BECKETT (BARTLETT) AL.

TEL BLDG.

WENTWORTH

SMOKEM HOP

JACKSON ST. TH.

PINCKNEY AL.

YUEN

BELLA UNION COOPER

1st 49-'06

GREAT CHINA

AH CHIC ACTOR

JAIL of '56

OLD HALL

ALL NAT'N.

DEVIL'S ACRE

DUNBAR AL.

MEZEPPA 1863

SENTINEL

5 POINTS

MORGUE '85

BATTLE ROW 80's

COPPA NO 2

Maguire's Theatre

MET. TH. 1854

RED MILL

MONTANA OLD HIPPODROME

PURCELLS

BOTTLE MEYER'S

PARENTI'S DIANA HALL

SPIDER KELLY

HIPPODROME

THALIA

BARBARY COAST ASBURY

133

BANK EXCHANGE

PUTNAMS SATYRS, NYMPHS

TEXAS TOMMY BUNNY HUG

TURKEY TROT

PISCO PUNCH
2 — 25¢ G.E.

CASCADES

SANGUINETTIE'S for
50¢

JESS JONES

DONG KING MAN

LIKE ONE HORSE SHAY

"If as they say,
God spawked the town
for being overfrisky.
Why did He burn the Churches down
and spare Hotaling's Whiskey?"
—Field

DINNER WITH WINE
1900's

1853 M.B.

OLD GROTTO

M

CHARCOAL FLAT IRON

APPRAISERS BLDG.

CHESS

COPYRIGHT 1947 K.G. CATHCART

CHINESE NEW YEAR
LION DANCE

魚肉

COMPASS INVENTED
SOUTH POINTING CHARIOT
CHINA
CA. 1000 BC

CHINATOWN

San Francisco's Chinatown has been commonly and historically referred to as the largest assemblage of people of Chinese ancestry living outside of China. While this might have changed over the past seventy or more years, what is certain is that despite the community's density and growth in San Francisco, those of Chinese ancestry were restricted to specific areas where they could work, live, and travel. It began with the Chinese Exclusion Act of 1882 and extended until the law was repealed in 1943.

Prior to 1882, San Francisco's Chinatown was a place of transition, with a small percentage of immigrants remaining and most others traveling elsewhere in California and the United States. After the completion of the railway in 1869 and California's delta in the 1870s, thousands of Chinese returned to San Francisco, triggering anti-Chinese sentiment and eventually leading to legislation blaming the Chinese for the economic slump and labor strife that naturally resulted from the completion of these great work projects. It is during this period that the most derogatory and negative stereotypes about the Chinese were created and promoted in the print media.

The known mapping history of San Francisco's Chinatown began with the notorious government map included in the 1885 Report of the Special Committee of the Board of Supervisors of San Francisco, known as the *Official Map of Chinatown in San Francisco*. This map, though rarely seen, is acknowledged by most Chinese Americans as the document that reinforced the legislative argument for the Chinese Exclusion Act.

Nothing noted on the Special Committee's map was illegal as of 1885, but everything was immoral, including gambling, prostitution, and opium. The creation of this map justified Chinese exclusion from the American dream, limiting travel and the rights to marry, work, and own land.

Everyone knew the map and it became a novelty, an attraction. Factually, it became a legitimate tourist map of San Francisco: anyone looking for the wrong thing to do could find it here. The tourism trade of the period included guided group visits to opium dens on Spofford Street and tours of the cow pens and slave markets on St. Louis Alley. Those looking for more individual attention often headed to the cribs for prostitutes, which were also well marked on the map.

The Committee's map served as the baseline for the reinforcement of negative stereotypes for generations to come. It is still well known by many San Franciscans, and you can occasionally find an original. Spec's Bar, a former joss house, lesbian bar, and merchant mariners' bar noted on the map, has a copy. It remains a powerful document revealing the violation of Chinese's constitutional rights prior to the repeal of the Chinese Exclusion Act in 1943. The Act eliminated virtually all immigration of Chinese citizens into the western United States and stood, in some form, from 1882 until the civil rights movement of 1964.

Cathcart's map, on the other hand, focuses on the rich culture, significant historic events, streets, buildings, and notable people of Chinatown. For example, the Tong Wars of the late 1800s—the violent disputes between rival fraternal factions—were significantly disrupted due to the 1906 earthquake and fire that destroyed most of Chinatown's opium dens, brothels, and gambling houses, but they soon rebuilt and their presence returned. By Cathcart's time, the

ABOVE: Cathcart's 1949 Map of San Francisco reflects early buildings and includes notes on life in the fifties. This map was his sixth creation and follows the proven method of surrounding a central map by vignettes related to the subject.

BELOW: This 1882 illustration from a German newspaper highlights what happened to gambling houses whose owners didn't pay off the police. In Chinatown, it was more often one tong paying the cops to thwart their competitors, or the raids were the result of a political offense to the white establishment.

recent tong troubles of the 1930s in San Francisco and New York City had settled down and were subdued, creating an environment safe to illuminate. Cathcart also pays homage to his host and sponsor, the Chinese Six Companies, which formed in the 1850s to assist Chinese immigrants subjected to racial discrimination and violence. Impressively, the Six Companies thrives to this day, boasting chapters in many large US cities. This dynamic backstory greatly aided Cathcart's work on the map and the quality of his photographs, many of which showcase local merchants and their families, businesses, and homes. At the same time, they document San Francisco's infamous Barbary Coast, reflecting the remnants of the notorious red-light district against the progressive and creative period of the 1940s.

The first section of the book focuses on Ken Cathcart's life and his time in San Francisco, featuring his never-before-seen early photographs of the city and exploring his interests. The second chapter explores Cathcart's map of Chinatown in detail, telling the story of San Francisco and Chinatown, and their interdependent development in the history of the Bay Area. The outer border of the map celebrates one hundred years of Chinese immigration to San Francisco and California while it contextualizes the culture and general background of Chinese immigrants. The inner grid delves into the more specific, deeper, often darker tales of Chinatown and the Barbary Coast heard by previous generations of San Franciscans, but unfamiliar today.

Gold Mountain, Big City takes the reader on a historical tour of San Francisco's Chinatown, revealing how the Chinese diaspora created the largest enclave outside of Asia and the oldest in the United States, and exploring the struggles, the triumphs, and the enduring legacy of these early immigrants.

Amerikanische Skizzen: Aufhebung einer chinesischen Spielhölle in San Francisco.

CHAPTER 1

KEN CATHCART

Artist, Mapmaker & Photographer, 1935–1955

1

KEN CATHCART: ARTIST, MAPMAKER & PHOTOGRAPHER, 1935–1955

L IKE SO MANY SAN FRANCISCO ENTHUSIASTS, Ken Cathcart was native to another place. Born Orene Gwin Cathcart in Harper, Kansas, in 1902, Cathcart grew up as a single child to Orion "Orie" Guthrie Cathcart, a musician, and Florence "Mattie" Gwin, an educator. The family owned a respected modern round cattle barn in their quaint Midwestern town, known for its famous water tower. Cathcart's classmates awarded him the "genius" designation upon his graduation from Winfield High School in 1921, believing he was destined to be an artist or scientist.

Cathcart began taking photos around 1924, around the time his mother became the dean of women at Harding College in Searcy, Arkansas. His subject matter included portraits of university students, family celebrations, and the rural scenery of the South during the Great Depression. He changed his name from Orene (a derivative of his father's name) to Kenneth Gwin when he moved to San Francisco in 1937 at the age of thirty-five. Was the name change sparked by a greater personal reinvention? We'll never know for certain, but moving to this new, artistic, diverse, and open-minded city may have motivated him to take on a persona separate from his conservative rural roots.

Before settling in San Francisco, Cathcart lived in Denver, Colorado, where he married and divorced quickly, and then briefly lived in Seattle.

Cathcart's photography provides valuable insight into his lifestyle, including a girlfriend who accompanied him around the city and destinations such as the Golden Gate International Exposition, Berkeley, and Seattle. But even Cathcart's nude photography seems distanced and more documentary-like than one would presume for a lover. Without knowledge of any descendants, we presume he was single for most of his life.

BELOW, TOP TO BOTTOM: This photo of a house in Searcy, Arkansas, shows power and phone lines passing overhead, but not connected. • The débutante cotillion shown here, held in a park in Searcy, features Cathcart's cousin (Cathcart, 1942).

COMING TO SAN FRANCISCO

San Francisco in 1937 was a vibrant place where Cathcart fit in naturally as a well-educated, working-class person. At this time in the city, there were jobs in logistics, manufacturing, processing, arts, and industry, as well as a growing class of white-collar banking, investment, public service, and commodities brokerages. Historically, the city also boasted a very strong wholesale and retail culture supported by the greater Northern California communities. It's probable that the publishing, printing, and artistic centers drew the young mapmaker to San Francisco, with readily available jobs in illustration, cartography, graphics, surveying, and ancillary industries. Cathcart may have been attracted to the availability of work, and though it wasn't high-paying employment, it was secure and plentiful, as was housing in his economic bracket.

What became immediately evident to us in Cathcart's photographs was his love of San Francisco and his thoroughly researched and well-documented capturing of the city he adopted and resided in from age thirty-five on. It was a treat to discover that among the first photos, as our introduction to Cathcart, were photos of him with his father on the day after Christmas in 1937, in his apartment at 1270 Pine Street, which was his first residence in San Francisco. He took still-life photographs documenting his one-room apartment, which was simply the dining room of a larger sectioned-off flat—the typical dining room wainscot familiar to San Franciscans next to the bed, his jacket hanging from the picture rail, built-in side hutch and cabinetry converted to pantry, and cabinets for a gas hot plate kitchen. He showed us the typical use of everyday items—the kitchen cupboard, the two-burner stove, the bags of sugar and coffee in commodity scale. We then see the equipment related to his brand-new Leica camera with which he shot most of his photographs in 40mm single-shot or 35mm rolled films as he continued to grow into a researcher, documentarian, and commercial photographer. These representations all helped us to date the time they were made in addition to the nature in which Cathcart lived, how he fed himself, how he spent his time. The photos show a man who lived a full but austere life. We imagine he lived like this until his death, forty-eight years after taking these initial San Francisco photographs.

By the time of the 1939 Golden Gate International Exposition, Cathcart had moved to 628 Montgomery Street, apartment 428, in a well-known building constructed in 1853 called the Montgomery Block. There, Cathcart

BELOW & FOLLOWING PAGES: Classic still lifes, in which Cathcart celebrated his new life in his first San Francisco residence on Pine Street, were favorite themes. Shot on his Leica camera, one image includes his previous camera in homage and adieu and another shows his sectioned-off living quarters (Cathcart, 1937). Also pictured is a self-portrait from his mother's house in Sacramento, California (Cathcart, 1944).

21

lived and worked among bohemians of the first order, including seventy-five or more documented artists supported by Works Progress Administration government funding.

Several of the artists working in the Montgomery Block area, and those living on nearby Telegraph Hill, became the "elite" bohemians, who worked on commissions or received

government subsidies. Among them were Bernard Zakheim, Ben Cunningham, Edith Hamlin, and Robert Stackpole, who worked on murals for Coit Tower; and John and Maury Logan Sloan, who created the Bohemian City Club murals.

The Montgomery Block, located where North Beach, the Barbary Coast, and the Financial District converge, was San Francisco's first fireproof building, a grand four-story block building of significant structure and great history. Originally named the "Washington Block," the building survived numerous early fires and epitomized the first settling of San Francisco and the pioneer spirit of the city's early inhabitants. It was also called the Monkey Block as homage to the "crazy" artists there.

ABOVE: This contemplative self-portrait may have been done with a timer on his new camera or perhaps with a remote shutter controller, as evidenced by the motion seen in his left hand (Cathcart, 1937).

OPPOSITE, CLOCKWISE FROM TOP LEFT: A view up to 13 Alta Street from the boardwalk of the Filbert Steps—a keen eye will note the longshoreman taking in the sights, looking east from the head of the stairway. • A toilet at 1360 Montgomery Street attests to the conditions in some parts of the city in 1937. • Unpainted and looking a bit tired, 13–31 Alta Street represented the housing of the working class, with number 27 being Cathcart's future home after 1958. (Cathcart, 1937).

In 1947, the year Cathcart's Chinatown map was published, there were "more artists and writers working in studios in this building than at any time in its history," according to O.P. Stidger, manager and immigration lawyer at the Montgomery Block. Cathcart occupied the same room, a single studio, from 1939 until a little before 1958, when the building was torn down. As a professional artist, Cathcart's live-work studio rented for fourteen dollars per month. During this time, he produced maps for the Rand McNally store on Market Street, although it appears that Cathcart never realized commercial success as a mapmaker. Cathcart's living and working in the Montgomery Block building may well have forged his relationship to the neighboring Chinatown, which later became central to his mapmaking work.

TELEGRAPH HILL IN THE 1930s

Ken Cathcart spent more than half of his life on Telegraph Hill. In the 1930s and earlier, this lively neighborhood was a bustling working-class area of immigrants, mostly living in humble homes and cottages, often unpainted, some built in the 1850s and 1860s. Telegraph Hill streets were without curbs and sidewalks (if they existed) were little more than dirt trails and created by necessity, covered by wood planks. The neighborhood's inhabitants were longshoremen, merchant seamen, ironworkers, artists, and a few true bohemians; the black sheep of the local wealthy families have always been evident, too. Shared, low-rent housing was plentiful, with seamen's cribs in basements and easy access to waterfront jobs and local iron yards. Many homes on the eastern slope during the 1920s and '30s still had outhouses and outdoor facilities for bathing. Hillside scars, left from rock quarrying activities years earlier, were still evident.

At this time, Telegraph Hill was part of the "Latin Quarter," a term implying an inhabitant whose first tongue is a Romance language, i.e., derived from Latin or Spanish colonial influence. Immigrants who shared Catholic roots, which included Irish families, joined the Italians from Lucca, Genoa, and Trieste, along with the Portuguese from Lisbon and the Azores, and the Spanish Basques. There were French Basques, Sicilians, and Sardinians as well. Restaurants in this central location of the Latin Quarter fed and housed the people working in the surrounding areas, just as it does today.

Interestingly, this area of Telegraph Hill and surrounding neighborhoods, with its diverse population, was, to a large extent, segregated. Chinatown was a place for "Orientals" to live, meaning not just Chinese, but all Asian people. They were segregated from the white Catholics of the Latin Quarter and the African Americans working and living in the cribs and joints of the Barbary Coast.

However, it also merits mentioning that despite the legislatively imposed segregation characteristic of this area, there were still a great number of Chinese Americans who grew up in the Latin Quarter.

All record of Cathcart's career as a mapmaker ends in 1958 with an unfinished manuscript map of San Francisco, in a three-by-four-foot format, larger than any of his previous maps. An article from 1957 in the *Semaphore*, a Telegraph Hill community paper, reports that Cathcart was working on a historic map of Telegraph Hill. This final, unfinished manuscript map, loosely based on United States Coastal Survey maps of San Francisco done from 1853 and 1859, appears to be a grand culmination of his previous productions. The working draft shows old and new shorelines and topography, including old racecourses and monuments related to historic events such as the 1915 Panama–Pacific International Exposition, cable-car lines, and old ships. The map follows the familiar Cathcart format with border spaces for vignettes surrounding the central map. Faint handwritten notations referencing historic facts, places, and names are visible on the draft.

What prevented Cathcart from completing and publishing this map? Why did he stop making maps altogether? We may never know for sure. More mysterious is the question of why there is no record of him between 1958 and the date of his death in 1985.

Without knowledge of any descendants or anyone still alive who knew him in his elder years, we can only guess. A brief conversation with his friend Laura indicated that he might have become blind.

What we know for sure is that Ken Cathcart lived among and documented many diverse ethnic communities as a true San Franciscan in the exciting years between 1937 and 1958. His body of work, including firsthand evidence, photographic record, notes, and personal references he left have been the best resources we've come across to chronicle the people, habits, and jobs of San Franciscans on Telegraph Hill and in Chinatown.

THE MAPPING HISTORY OF CHINATOWN

The cataclysmic earthquake and fire of 1906 changed Chinatown forever.

It took more than a year to clean up and begin reconstruction of Chinatown, in part because of a serious fight from politicians, businesses, and others who had long proposed moving the neighborhood from one of the city's most desirable locations to the mudflats on the southern outskirts of the city. In the end, Chinatown stayed where it was, but not without significant changes to its buildings and well-known underworld. Post-earthquake

OPPOSITE, TOP TO BOTTOM: Cathcart's 1946 Sketch Map of California Gold Region, with Notes and Memorabilia, Chiefly of the Golden Era is a nod to Bret Harte's Golden Era *newspaper from San Francisco in the 1860s. • The Punnett Brothers' 1907 map depicting San Francisco one year after the fire shows each newly issued permit and the related reconstruction for a city being rebuilt. The red line is the reaches of the fire.*

ABOVE: Cathcart's map of San Francisco history includes the original shoreline with present shoreline overlay, full topography and riparian information, early railroads, horse race tracks, and numerous details extracted from the 1853, 1857, and 1869 US Coast Survey maps produced by the federal government. Likely his most ambitious work, it remained incomplete.

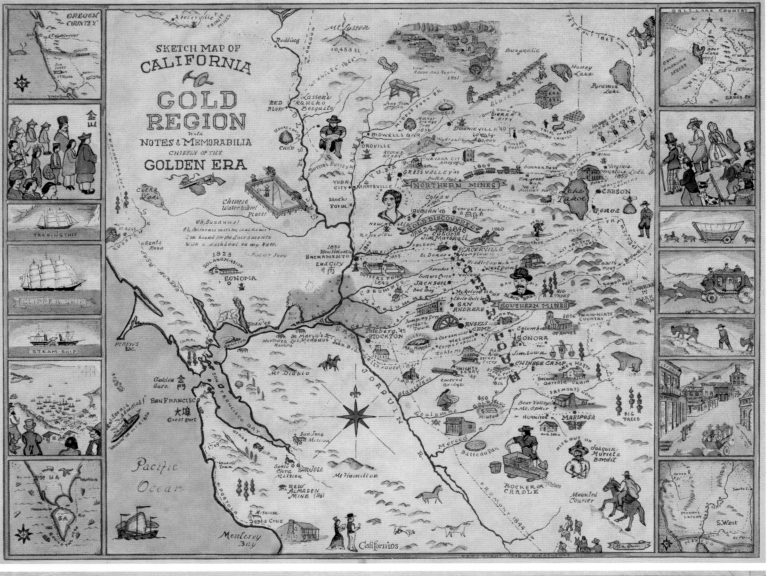

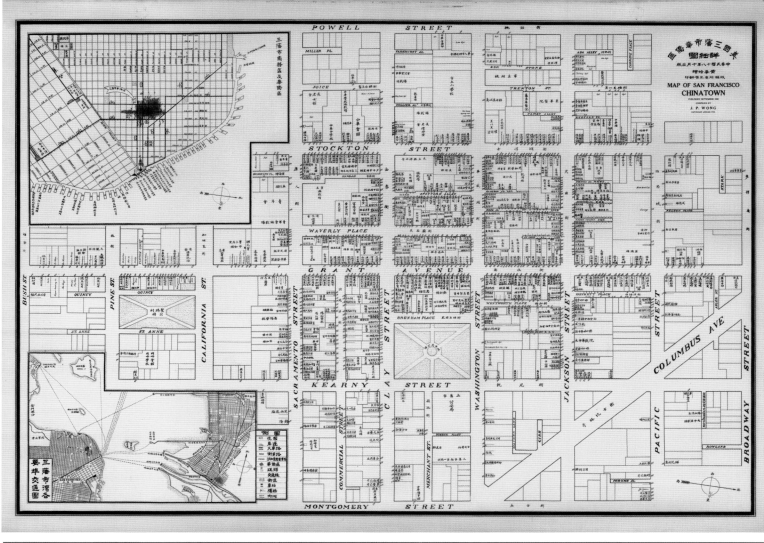

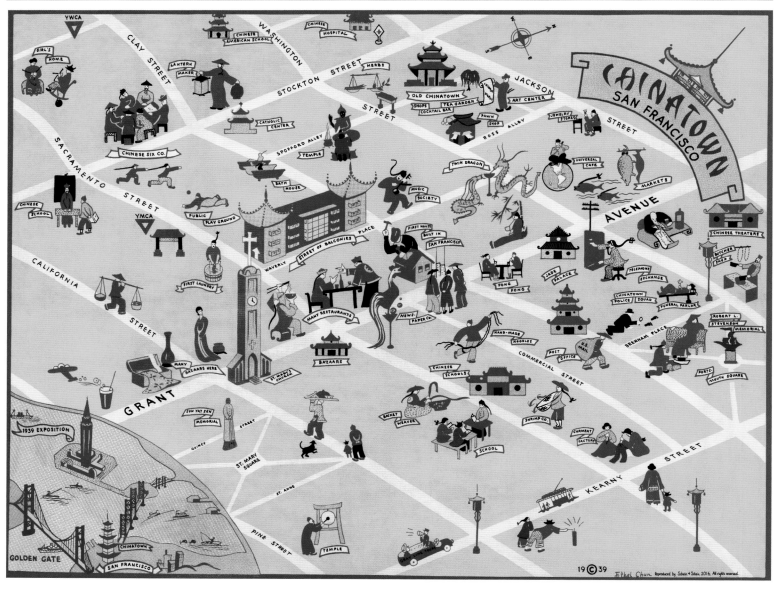

construction projects were commissioned by Chinatown leaders using Western architects to materialize a fantasy of China for visiting tourists, and though some vice activities continued, the majority of the slave markets, opium dens, and Pacific Avenue underground passageways were not rebuilt, severely limiting those activities for years to come.

Prior to the earthquake, there were few to no promotional maps, only the 1885 exclusion map, after which business and tourist interests successfully promoted Chinatown through maps on business cards showing their individual location. At the beginning of the twentieth century, a few influential authors, artists, mapmakers, photographers, and media writers began documenting Chinatown in a more positive light with books and photos, but also with an eye toward economic promotion.

One notable map from this period was produced in 1929 by the Six Companies, a benevolent organization working on behalf of Chinese and Chinese Americans. The J.P. Wong map was created to celebrate the growth of Chinatown and the growing American-born Chinese community in the Bay Area.

Like the Exclusion Act map, the J.P. Wong map lists the uses of most spaces within Chinatown but targets their own community by using mostly Chinese characters. An English translation of the map was produced and may still survive somewhere. Unfortunately, the J.P. Wong map did not enjoy significant commercial success because Chinese and American-born Chinese did not consider its black-and-white appearance to be celebratory or appropriate.

The J.P. Wong map is believed to have been a small version of a larger map displayed at the Six Companies building. The map features extended boundaries of the neighborhood and includes two inserts of the Bay Area, including fishing camps and Oakland. It also shows the immigration station on Angel Island, which was dedicated to enforcing the Exclusion Act in the western United States and where both returning Chinese Americans and new Chinese immigrants waited before joining family or hosts in Chinatown.

In 1939, Ethel Chun and the California Chinese Pioneer Historical Society produced a map of Chinatown to serve as a tourist guide to direct the tens of thousands of visitors traveling to San Francisco for the Golden Gate International Exposition (GGIE) that year. Although rudimentary, the map is bright, colorful, and happy, and very much in keeping with the illustrative style of the period. Cathcart may well have seen it on one of his three visits to the Chinese Village at the GGIE, as the photo record reflects. It's notable that many of California's Chinatown families performed as dancers and thespians or acted as presenters, artisans, and cultural liaisons at the exposition events.

Other non-Chinese Americans, such as Will Irwin, Arnold Genthe, Charles Caldwell Dobie, and E.H. Suydam, have also explored the history and culture of San Francisco's Chinatown with their art. Cathcart used these authors' works as archetypes and applied them to his mapmaker perspectives (documented by photography) with the express purpose of creating an honest representation. In Chinatown, that perspective was from the point of view of a foreigner. Cathcart's work shows he understood that his approach as an outsider required a focus grounded in a positive portrayal of the Chinese in America, including the importance of Dr. Sun Yat-sen to the Chinese community and the importance of the repeal of the Exclusion Act, both as written about by Dr. Poon Chew, the publisher the first Chinese-language daily newspaper outside of China. It is important to remember that Cathcart's map was made for promotional purposes, so his approach was not that of a historian, but rather that of an artist hired to create a marketing piece for tourists.

During Cathcart's time living near Chinatown, he was perhaps one of the more involved non-Asian San Franciscans ever to comprehensively research the subject of Chinatown. His ten-year photographic record of the neighborhood clearly reveals a man welcomed and granted access to family homes, culture, and community, even though he was an outsider.

Research indicates that Cathcart's introduction to Chinatown, the Chinese American community, and even his newly adopted city of San Francisco came through the patronage of B.S. Fong and family, and others in the Six Companies. Also known as the Chinese Consolidated Benevolent Association (CCBA), the Six Companies was founded in the 1850s by representatives of six prominent Chinese families to address the needs of Chinese immigrants. These community leaders and their families are featured in portraits taken by Cathcart rather early in his time in San Francisco, between the years of 1937 and 1938.

The Fongs' supportive role in the Chinese War Relief Association of America is something that may have required marketing, promotion, and documentation in order to raise money and spread awareness of the war-relief campaign. This was a perfect job for a photographer, aspiring author/wordsmith, and illustrator like Cathcart. The mapmaker's own textual descriptions of these formal photographs imply a professional relationship forged with the Fongs and others of the Six Companies. In addition, Mr. Fong's numerous other activities as director of the Louie Fong Kwong Association, a member of the Chinatown chamber of commerce executive committee, representative for United and American Airlines in Chinatown, and president of an import/export store provided excellent references and an important Chinatown host. All of this may have helped Cathcart gain access not commonly granted to others outside of the Chinese community.

Despite certain superficialities of his work, Cathcart clearly engaged with Chinatown's leaders, residents, and wide-ranging communities in a respectful and celebratory manner.

LEFT: *This proud donor poses with middle-school girls gathered in front of the Great China Theatre, collecting for the Chinese War Relief Fund, which Cathcart was hired to document (Cathcart, 1937–38).*

OPPOSITE: *This shoeshine boy on Grant Avenue, with a shine box homemade from crates, is emblematic of kids who worked in Chinatown. Always ready for promotion, these young go-getters were frequently the children of merchants in Chinatown and always residents (Cathcart, 1937).*

CHAPTER 2

THE MAP'S OUTER GRID

Chinese History & America's First Chinatown

2

A PRIMER FOR READING CATHCART'S CHINATOWN MAP

THE 177 SPACES ON CATHCART'S MAP represent the same number of stories. Of these spaces, twenty-six are vignettes arranged around the border of the map. They are organized in a grid consisting of an outside perimeter that is ordered alphabetically. The interior icons are arranged in a grid with A through G serving as the y-axis coordinates, and the numerical coordinates of 1 through 9 serve as the x-axis.

Cathcart meticulously placed icons on the map with a great deal of care and technical accuracy in his research. The vast majority of the map's icons also have a corresponding photographic reference. Cathcart took more than a thousand photographs of Chinatown from 1936 to 1946—more material than any other known artist has collected about Chinatown during this ten-year period. Cathcart's photographs became the fundamental documentation from which he designed and built his maps, including street scenes, shop windows, and portraits of people living and working in and around Chinatown.

The descriptions for these icons are intended as intriguing facts to captivate the curiosity of readers. Many of the subjects in these icons have driven great interest in this map ever since it was first produced in 1947. Of course, there are still details cryptic or vague enough that we haven't been able to decipher them.

We believe that the majority of the illustrations were drawn from Ken Cathcart's imagination (with the exception of references to Genthe photographs). They are representations of what he thought was important about Chinatown to outsiders and what was reviewed by the Chinese American community, which he had engaged with and documented for the previous ten years.

Cathcart's map of Chinatown was made using a laborious hand-drawn photolithographic process. This was a very specialized approach during this mid-century period of history and mapmaking. It was technologically advanced for its time, but time-consuming. Cathcart cut out the drawings and created a collage in the form of a scrapbook, calling it a "scrapbook map." Simply put, scrapbook maps were created by cutting and pasting illustrations, photographing them, and then reducing the images. Cathcart even used white paint, long before the invention of "white-out," to hide flaws or create outlines and boundaries for some of his drawings.

Within the map area, the majority of icons tell the story of the current body politic, daily life on the street, Chinatown business, Chinese family life, and the historic events, places, and materials that make up the foundation of Chinatown as a community in San Francisco. In addition to these celebratory icons and stories, Cathcart included business associations who, at the time and/or historically, had contributed to these story outlines in a violent, exploitive, or negative manner. From involvement in the Tong Wars of the 1880s to the 1930s to groups trading in sex slaves, prostitutes, opium,

BELOW: This view of a parade down Grant Avenue, as seen from the balcony of the Hang Far Low restaurant, reveals a glimpse of the street grid reflected in the heart of Cathcart's map (Cathcart, 1938).

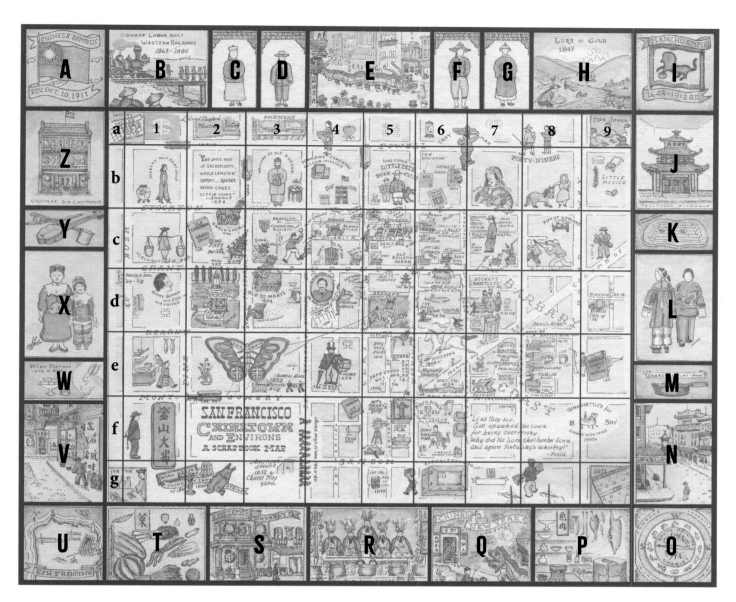

ABOVE: Cathcart's 1947 pictorial map of Chinatown tells the stories of the people, daily life on the street, business, family life, historic events, and places of the largest Chinese community outside of Asia.

The overlay of letters and numbers pictured here corresponds to text throughout the book, which explains what each icon or vignette is depicting. The outer border is ordered alphabetically (with capital letters) and the icons of the inner map are identified by a coordinate grid. For example, "b1" explains the significance of the urn and the slit-skirt dress. Return to this map for reference as you make your way through the book.

gambling, extortion, and "protection" rackets, these historical references contribute to the greater overall story—and these problems transpired as a result of Chinese exclusion and isolation, as well as a lack of law-and-order support from San Francisco and America to combat them in an evenhanded manner with community representation. This map was intended as a positive portrayal and celebration of Chinatown, so it's odd for us to see some things that make us cringe today, but at the time, they were nonoffensive or even considered acceptable due to cultural ignorance (or, alternatively, politely overlooked). The map Cathcart produced was an honest attempt to express the depth of the Chinese American culture in San Francisco.

It's likely that Cathcart's map is the result of his fascination with Dobie and Suydam's book *Chinatown*, possibly published in the Montgomery Block in 1936, before he arrived in San Francisco. Some of the illustrations, as well as the book itself, are referenced on the map. Herbert Asbury's book, *The Barbary Coast*, was published in 1933 and also appears on the map. These books were greatly influential and perhaps even motivated Cathcart to move to San Francisco in the first place.

Even though the map mostly includes icons directly related to Chinese American life and history, it also shows many other early San Francisco venues and landmarks, such as theaters, the Poodle Dog restaurant, the California Theater, Parrott's Granite Block (built by Chinese laborers with stone brought from China), and the *Niantic* buried ship.

The Barbary Coast, also an important neighborhood, is included on the map because of its close proximity to Chinatown and the timeline it shared. The history of the Montgomery Block and Barbary Coast is evident through their iconography and stories as well as the photographs that accompany them. Subsequent research at the California Historical Society revealed to us that Cathcart's failed attempts to publish his books provided him with an excellent framework for making historic maps. His unpublished crib sheets are the foundations of his historic maps.

We recognize that the details can't help but be skewed by the perspective and privileges afforded him as an outsider. That said, we also believe that the Chinese community approved of this map as an appropriate marketing device to promote postwar Chinatown to white American tourists and San Franciscans. Eventually, the community representation became a story of success in attaining recognition and political representation as Chinese and as Americans. The repeal of the Exclusion Act in 1943 was a big first step and a true cause for celebration. No greater, more important, more impactful event would transpire for Chinese Americans—nationwide, but particularly in San Francisco—until the civil rights movement of the 1960s, which eliminated the discriminatory laws still remaining after the Act was repealed.

We didn't find any of Cathcart's photographs of Chinatown taken after the map was published. What we did find in his collection were photographs representative of commercial work, consisting of family association portraits and private commercial photos for the remainder of his working life from 1947 to 1958.

The work on this map, both text and coloring, involved two years of working with a single sepia-toned artist's proof Cathcart made from a photolithographic plate (both of which we have in the collection), and then having it hand-colored. The hand-coloring was done, in part, because the sepia-toned proof lacked blacks, dark tones, and any color, but iconographically, it was fascinating.

By great fortune, Ellen Cox, a watercolorist whom we believe is one of the best in the world, agreed to work on Cathcart's map and really helped make the creation of this map possible. Once it was hand-colored, we handed it off to our Photoshop expert, Alex Jeongco, who cleaned up the map, resized and color-enhanced it, and newly copyrighted the reproduction to us.

It wasn't until after coloring the map that we learned that Cathcart had created a colored artist's proof of his Chinatown map, which is currently housed in the California Historical Society's collection. Whoever colored the map appeared to have used a mixture of watercolor and pencil or crayon. Our hope is that San Franciscans of different ages will see the map and, with their varied interests, motivations, and love for our city's history, recognize illustrations that we have not yet deciphered.

OPPOSITE: *This is a view of the Mechanics' Institute, which is the oldest library in the western United States and a primary site of Cathcart's in-depth research on San Francisco history (Cathcart, 1946).*

LEFT: *Sitting on the corner of Clay Street and Grant Avenue, the Soo Yuen Benevolent Association Building houses the organization that the Louis, Fong, and Kwong families founded in 1846, which was set up to provide aid to members of these three families. Cathcart's Chinatown host and employer B.S. Fong was the president of the organization from 1936 to 1946 (Cathcart, 1937).*

THE BORDER OF CATHCART'S MAP highlights Chinese immigration to San Francisco, along with its causes and effects, as well as the people and their costumes, work, community, lifestyle, and festivals. Overall, it represents San Francisco history from 1847 to 1947 through the lives of San Franciscans of Chinese descent. All of his drawings of the icons and surrounding vignettes of buildings and scenes were made in a larger working scale, roughly twelve inches tall, which was then reduced photolithographically.

A **CHINESE REPUBLIC 1912, REV. OCT. 10, 1911:** Formation of the Chinese Republic in 1912 followed the Xinhai Revolution on October 10, 1911. Prior to its formation, China was ruled by the Qing Dynasty (aka the Manchu Empire in box I), which was overthrown in this revolution. This was relevant to the residents of Chinatown, due to the generally unfavorable sentiment toward the political environment and pervasive poverty in China. Parades on October 10 were common into the '50s, in celebration of the revolution and the creation of China's only democratic constitution.

B **CHINESE LABOR BUILT WESTERN RAILROADS, 1863–1880:** The Chinese immigrant, as a skilled or unskilled laborer, was in demand by Leland Stanford for the construction of the Central Pacific Railroad. Not mentioned, and of more interest to us for its lack of recognition, was the use of existing Chinese pump-and-drain technology to tame the California Delta between 1860 and the early 1880s. (See also box a2.)

    **C D F G**

NINETEENTH-CENTURY COSTUMES: These outfits are directly associated with four nonexcluded trades, or jobs the Chinese could have in the United States (as per the Exclusion Act), that were also honorable in Chinese culture: merchant (C), laborer (D), farmer (F), and scholar (G). The problem with this representation is that only two of the four figures are properly dressed. The farmer and laborer have calf-length pants and field slippers, but the merchant's and scholar's robes aren't long enough and the shoes are inaccurate. Cathcart also invented the hats, which may show a lack of understanding of the subtle interpretations of rank and position emphasized in Chinese costumes. Despite this modification, the intent is easily understood.

OPPOSITE, TOP TO BOTTOM: Chinese laborers were a large part of the Central Pacific workforce that built the transcontinental railroad. The influx of Chinese immigrants, which was considered a threat to the status quo, led to the enactment of the 1882 Chinese Exclusion Act, which not only barred immigration, but denied work and imposed taxes on the community.
• This engraving from 1895 portrays Chinese merchants in traditional attire.

LEFT: Bedecked in traditional clothes and carrying a pipe, this man plays host at the entrance to the theater of the Chinese Village at the GGIE, which employed many Chinatown residents during its run (Cathcart, 1939).

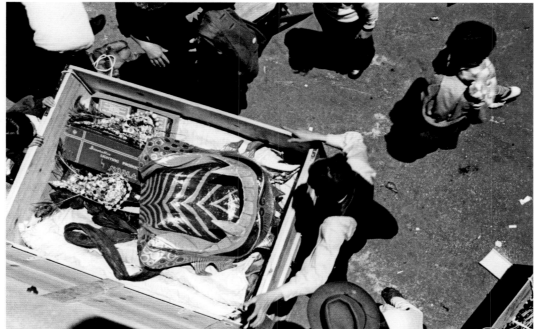

E **CHINESE NEW YEAR DRAGON DANCE:** The dragon, an auspicious symbol of power, wisdom, and good fortune, chases away evil spirits and brings happiness, longevity, and good luck. New Year's or spring celebrations are when it is most often seen, but weddings or the openings of stores are good places to spot one, too. It is usually accompanied by flutes, drums, firecrackers, and a group of dancers. (See also box Q.)

RIGHT: *The dragon dance has been used in Chinese festivals since ancient times. Here, Cathcart captures the opening of the crate, revealing the dragon that awaits its awakening by skilled dancers and puppeteers (Cathcart, 1938).*

OPPOSITE: *This French map from 1849, depicting accurate riparian and topographic information, was the best tool of its time to locate the mines. The map delineates silver and gold mines, the J.C. Fremont route, John Sutter's New Helvetia, and Tulare Lake.*

H **LURE OF GOLD, 1849:** This graphic depicts a Chinese miner. Merchant William Heath Davis wrote that a Chinese man and woman arrived on the brig *Eagle* on February 2, 1848, the first to appear in the port of San Francisco. During that winter, the number of Chinese immigrants increased rapidly. Getting passage to Stockton and from there to the mines was another challenge because they didn't speak the language and were not familiar with Western ways. Businessman Thomas O. Larkin received a letter on March 6, 1848, revealing that Chinese immigrants had an advocate in Charles V. Gillespie, who said that he enjoyed introducing Chinese immigrants into this country.

MANCHU EMPIRE, 1644–1912 A.D.: The Manchu, also known as the Qing dynasty, maintained imperial rule before the Republic of China was established in 1912. (The actual fall of the Qing dynasty occurred on October 10, 1911, but the emperor only officially abdicated in early 1912, so the date has been listed accordingly.) From the 1850s through the 1870s, the majority of immigrants from China were fleeing poverty under this regime. This was a result of the taxation of China after the British won the Opium Wars and demanded reparations along with the continued purchase of their opium. This led to the collapse of the Chinese monarchy and feudal system, and consequently mass starvation, largely causing the exodus of its peoples to California.

TELEPHONE BUILDING: This was the site of the telephone exchange, operating from 1894 to 1949. Access to the regular phone system was withheld from Chinese as part of the Exclusion Act. It was designed to prevent employment in specific trades along with other ancillary support industries, which included segregating telephone operators and operation locations within the community it served. Despite these exclusive origins, its operators were known for their ingenuity, effectiveness, intelligence, and spatial memory. This structure was built in China, prefabricated, disassembled, and brought to San Francisco for the exclusive purpose of housing the telephone switchboard exchange for Chinatown. The building itself was built as a fitted post-and-beam wooden construction exemplary of the Canton region of China in which it was produced, and is probably the only truly Chinese-designed building in Chinatown, as opposed to an Americanized rendering. (See also box d5.)

OPPOSITE: The Chinatown Telephone Exchange was built in the style of a three-tiered pagoda. Still operating at the time of this photo, the company would become obsolete with the advent of dial phones in the late 1940s (Cathcart, 1938).

162 Chinese Telephone Office San Francisco-California Destroyed by earthquake and fire Apr. 18. 1906.

LEFT: This 1906 postcard shows Chinatown Telephone Exchange operators, who fielded hundreds of calls per day and had to know where every family lived, their address, members of their family's relationship with each other, businesses related to the family, and, of course, everybody's name— all to be employed within seconds of receiving the call.

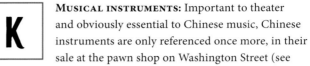

MUSICAL INSTRUMENTS: Important to theater and obviously essential to Chinese music, Chinese instruments are only referenced once more, in their sale at the pawn shop on Washington Street (see box c6). All the theater scenes and many of the charity events are musically oriented, but this is not as comprehensively covered, despite its cultural importance. (See also box Y.)

LEFT, TOP TO BOTTOM: This window display on Grant Avenue showcases traditional Chinese instruments, each of which produces a unique sound, and many of which can trace their roots to several thousand years ago. • This harmonica band is performing at a 1938 war relief event at the Great China Theatre. (Cathcart, 1938.)

FAR RIGHT & BELOW:
Arnold Genthe, who
took hundreds of pho-
tographs of pre-1906
Chinatown, offered
rare glimpses into an
often demonized and
misunderstood culture.
Here, his images were
used on postcards to
promote Chinatown
after the earthquake,
thus reinforcing
Chinese Americans'
rightful place in a
newly reconstructed
San Francisco.

L **CHILDREN OF OLD CHINATOWN:** The costumes associated with Chinese Americans were very different from those of Europeans. Celebrations among Chinese such as the New Year, christenings, and family events were regarded as occasions to wear such patterns and designs. Cathcart based his illustrations on photographs by Arnold Genthe.

" CHILDREN WERE THE PRIDE, JOY,
BEAUTY AND CHIEF DELIGHT
OF THE QUARTER "

M **CHARCOAL FLAT IRON:** Ironing work, as part of the greater laundry business, was a very important service. It allowed for a pristine, starched shirt and collar at a time when roads were dusty and people lacked good personal hygiene. Chinese laundries impressed Westerners greatly with this crisp, ironed look. The Chinese community turned ironing into a promotional success well into the 1970s, with an expectation of the highest standards for laundering and pressing.

LEFT: This photograph depicts one of the few places that existed to represent Chinese Americans when the law otherwise didn't. That there was a Chinese laundry union office was a surprise, but understandable given San Francisco's pro-labor sentiments— despite the Chinese Exclusion Act, even the Chinese could unionize (Cathcart, 1942).

OPPOSITE: This laundry worker, holding linens for a local hotel or restaurant, is representative of what was considered honorable work, readily available and commonly family-operated (Cathcart, 1938).

OPPOSITE: *This image of the Four Families building on the 900 block of Grant Avenue illustrates Cathcart's use of photography to create illustrations for his maps (Cathcart, 1938).*

BELOW: *Cathcart referenced the photos of the lamppost going through an awning on Grant Avenue for his map illustration (Cathcart, 1938).*

N **STREET SCENE:** This is Grant Avenue at Washington Street, looking north toward the Four Families building (see also box d6). This is another scene drawn from real life with an identifiable location and a traditionally dressed person to suggest an earlier age. It is also a direct homage to Suydam's illustration of the same location in his 1936 book, *Chinatown*.

O **SOUTH POINTING CHARIOT, *CHINAN CHE*:** The phrase *chinan che* means "south-facing chariot." Its invention is attributed to the Chinese, but when it was invented is disputed, with sources ranging between 1000 BCE and 200 CE. Regardless of its origins, it was a two-wheeled vehicle with a device used to point south at all times. How exactly it worked has been lost to history, but it was capable of georeferencing mechanically rather than magnetically, with a figure standing on top of the chariot always moving to compensate for the change in direction of the cart, always keeping a southern face. The device could be set up to face any compass direction, but south was the traditional choice.

P **KITCHEN SCENE WITH FISH, GAME, PIGS, AND KNIVES:** This was attributed to the prepared-foods culture of Chinatown, as delivered by a "tray man" (see box a6). The idea of finished food, to be removed and eaten elsewhere, was unheard of in Euro-American culture prior to 1860 as far as we can tell. We believe that, living in the Montgomery Block, these services were essential to Cathcart's daily life. Interestingly, the Chinese characters, while accurate, are translated literally rather than used to create meaning.

LEFT: *This pensive shot shows a man, who is unusually fit for the day, boxing duck at Goong Chew to provide food for neighbors working long hours. This business model has spread to urban areas nationwide (Cathcart, 1938).*

Q **DRAGON PARADE:** In Chinese culture, the dragon, the presence of which dates back to the fifth millennium BC, is often used as a symbol to represent imperial strength and power. (See also box E.)

ABOVE RIGHT, RIGHT & BELOW: These examples of dragon heads were taken from local celebrations on the 1100 block of Stockton Street. The sections that make up the dragon were originally constructed of wood, with a series of connected bamboo hoops covered in rich fabrics. (Cathcart, 1938.)

R **IN OLD JOSS HOUSE:** A "joss house" is an old English term for a Chinese temple or shrine. Incense was burned in front of or inside these buildings. This entry depicts five figures or deities on the temple altar inside the Tin How Temple, which was very similar to one publicly displayed at the Golden Gate International Exposition. (See also box S.)

BELOW: Temples are the center of many family celebrations outside the home (Cathcart, 1939).

BELOW: Families focus on traditional and regional stories of the virtues of living a life of the bodhisattva, or moving in the direction of the Buddha, through prayer and meditation (Cathcart, 1939).

S   **OLD TEMPLE, WAVERLY PL.:** This is a reference to the elaborate Tin How Temple at Waverly Place, which some claim is the oldest privately owned Chinese temple in the United States. It is celebrated for these facts and the success of its followers. (See also box c5.)

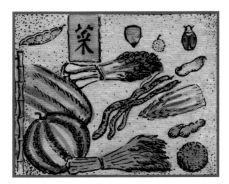

T

FRESH VEGETABLES: The Chinese brought with them a culture of cultivating and selling fresh produce. Early settlers of San Francisco lacked access to greens and their diets were poor as a result, so fresh produce was a new concept. These foods were accessible, cheap, delicious, and nutritious, sold from vendors' carts or specialized merchants' stalls. Chinese exclusion laws did not restrict manual labor and farming, so many Chinese immigrants took to farming as an honorable way of making a living.

FAR LEFT & LEFT: These newspaper engravings are realistic representations of local dress, customs, and retail endeavors of the day.

U

INSET MAP OF SAN FRANCISCO SHOWING MAP AREA: This map shows Chinatown in relation to the Mission San Francisco de Asís, the newly constructed Golden Gate Bridge, and windmills in Golden Gate Park. It is similar to the J.P. Wong map (see page 28), as it includes both the area at large and the outlining identification of Chinatown as a central element of the greater San Francisco scene. This little map is unusual among Cathcart's maps to represent the entire city in context, the other example of this format being his incomplete 1958 manuscript map.

V

END OF COMMERCIAL STREET AT GRANT AVENUE, WITH HANG FAR LOW IN BACKGROUND: This scene is taken from real life, in that Cathcart's photos show the restaurant and surrounding buildings, but most of the characters on the wall are fake. A remnant of 1940s bias, Cathcart did not attempt to depict accurate representations of Chinese writing. Rather, using artistic license, he illustrated an identifiable location with no greater purpose than to celebrate its charm and create an impressionistic view.

MOON FESTIVAL, 15TH OF 8TH: The Moon Festival, also known as the Mid-Autumn Festival, occurs on the fifteenth day of the eighth month of the Chinese lunar calendar. Its main purpose is to give thanks for a good harvest, so special foods, such as the mid-autumn moon cakes shown here, take center stage for this event. The rabbit refers to an ancient Chinese legend about the "moon hare," who lives on the moon.

CHILDREN OF OLD CHINATOWN: This is another homage to the early twentieth-century style of dress. It was rarely used as everyday wear at the time of this map's creation, seen only during holidays and at family events. Arnold Genthe's 1903 photographs of Chinatown were patriarchal and perhaps patronizing, but were the first effective attempt to soften the negative anti-Chinese rhetoric of the 1880s and humanize a previously demonized culture by showing the Chinese appreciation for their children and other aspects of family life.

RIGHT: This postcard of Chinatown children gazing directly into the camera attempts to emulate Genthe's street scenes, but perhaps with less mystery or lyricism.

MUSICAL INSTRUMENTS: An *erhu*, a two-stringed bowed musical instrument, is pictured underneath a plucked string instrument, a stylized *ruan*, both of which are commonly used by theater bands and street performers. (See also box K.)

CHINESE SIX COMPANIES

Z **CHINESE SIX COMPANIES:** The Six Companies was originally founded in San Francisco to protect the interests of Chinese immigrants, since the American government offered them little to no protections. It was made up of six family associations: Kong Chow, Ning Yeung, Sam Yup, Yeong Wo, Hop Wo, and Yan Wo. The Six Companies was instrumental in providing basic services to their community, including helping to take care of the sick and the poor, setting up a Chinese-language school, maintaining a Chinese census, and assisting the Chinese coming from and going to China, as well as returning corpses to China for burial. It also provided legal help and protection against the rampant discrimination and racism, and it played a significant role in the financing and reconstruction of Chinatown after the 1906 earthquake and fire. The Six Companies was well known to the white community of San Francisco. As an organization that promoted business, it was frequently in communication with

downtown merchants in the nineteenth and twentieth centuries. It was through the Six Companies that Leland Stanford hired Chinese labor for his railroad. The Six Companies also produced the J.P. Wong Chinatown map in 1929 (see page 28). For Cathcart, his first employment opportunity and introduction to Chinatown was with the Six Companies, through B.S. Fong. The building in Cathcart's map is a depiction of its headquarters. (See also box b4.)

LEFT: Politicizing available street views is nothing new, as is evidenced by the anti-Japan bomb poster in the background of this local shop (Cathcart, 1938).

BELOW: This gathering of the China War Relief Association of America (CWRAA) and supporters at the Chinese Consolidated Benevolent Association (CCBA) and the Six Companies meeting hall on Stockton Street features B.S. Fong (center at the end of the table; Cathcart, 1937).

OPPOSITE: This photo of the Six Companies Building on Stockton Street, with a banner declaring it the site of the CWRAA headquarters, summarizes Cathcart's reason for being here and the impetus behind his Chinatown map's creation (Cathcart, 1937).

CHAPTER 3

THE MAP'S INNER GRID

Chinatown & Barbary Coast Tales

3

DAILY LIFE IN THE NOTORIOUS NEIGHBORHOOD

WHILE THE ICONS ON THE OUTSIDE OF THE GRID outline the history and culture of Chinese immigrants in general, the interior icons are devoted to telling the stories about Chinatown's community, its people, daily life on the street, business, family life, historical events, and places that help establish the foundation of San Francisco's Chinatown community. In addition to these positive icons and stories, Cathcart also included stories that were violent and exploitative, involving tong business associations. The Tong Wars of the 1880s to the 1930s were internecine disputes involving rival tong factions, who controlled underworld activities, such as gambling and prostitution. These historical references provide the reader with complex, multilayered stories, some resulting from Chinatown's isolation and lack of law and order due to the Exclusion Act.

a1

LOTTERY LUCK CO.: It seems common today, but lotteries used to be illegal because they were a form of gambling. The only exceptions were churches in which bingo or lottery games were played. The Chinese numbers lottery was controlled within the community, with white San Francisco unable to regulate or graft it. Postings along Grant and Clay Streets or the bulletin board (see box c6) on Washington Street alerted the winners.

UNKNOWN ICON: We were unable to decipher the meaning of this symbol.

a2

LELAND STANFORD MANSION: Railroad baron Leland Stanford established this residence, located at California and Powell, in 1857. In a letter Stanford wrote to President Polk, he expressed his support of Chinese laborers for their work ethic and reasonable nature. Stanford hired Chinese laborers to build his Central Pacific Railroad track and beds, despite heated objections from competing railroads and their supporters.

a3

FAIRMONT, 1906–9: The Fairmont Hotel, located at California and Powell, was in the final stages of completion when the earthquake and fire of 1906 severely damaged its interior and delayed its opening until 1907. It still stands on Nob Hill today with additions such as a tower overlooking Chinatown.

OPPOSITE, TOP TO BOTTOM: The Leland Stanford Mansion, built between 1856 and 1857, was purchased in 1861 by Leland Stanford, before he became California's eighth governor. Stanford, who founded Stanford University in his son's memory, expanded the original two-story house to four stories. • The Fairmont Hotel, pictured here shortly after the 1906 earthquake and fire, was repaired by notable architect Julia Morgan, who was exploring innovative techniques such as using reinforced concrete so that buildings could withstand earthquakes.

No. 120. Residence of Governor Stanford, San Francisco, Cal.

a4

CHILD DRESSED IN OLD GARB: This simple drawing illustrates traditional clothing, which was still evident in Cathcart's time, particularly on children dressed for special occasions, such as New Year's, or on old-timers who carried the tradition to the end. An homage to Genthe, it was Cathcart's reminder to respect the old ways.

232. Po and Wing, Chinatown, San Francisco, Cal.

LEFT: Derived from Genthe's photos, this type of ephemeral imagery was popular from around 1900 to 1935 and is credited with helping to humanize Chinatown.

JADE HEART ICON: Revered in Chinese culture for six thousand years, jade's meaning varies with the type, but its beauty and power to create tranquility are universally acknowledged. Jadeite, a rare form associated with health, longevity, and love, is said to open one's heart when used for meditation, which Cathcart may have been alluding to here.

RIGHT, TOP TO BOTTOM: A jade carver displays his skill in a workshop, which was moved from Chinatown to the GGIE Chinese Village to display and promote the artistry to the public (Cathcart, 1939).
• A Grant Avenue window display showcases imported jade artifacts. Deemed the highest quality available nationwide, these examples would qualify as museum pieces today (Cathcart, 1937).

a5

SYMBOL OF DOUBLE HAPPINESS: Each half of this character is the sign for happiness; put together, it is double happiness, representing unity in a successful marriage. This symbol is still seen at most Chinese wedding receptions today.

a6

CHINESE VASE: This is an acknowledgment of the origins of China and the quality of goods sold within Chinatown on Grant Avenue, particularly ceramics. Urns and vases have ceremonial functions, so form, color, and application have influence on its status in context. Like flowers, the proper urn or vase matters. (See also box b1.)

FAR LEFT & LEFT: Cathcart staged a great number of photo shoots to highlight Chinatown wares and the merchants who sold them. These examples are among two hundred such photographs (Cathcart, 1937).

TRAY MAN: The delivery man was something every Chinese restaurant had for those who couldn't eat at the restaurant. There were dozens of men employed in this manner along Jackson and Clay Streets and Grant Avenue. The map shows a man with a queue, a hairstyle that represents an earlier time than our photographic period. Chinese food was the only cuisine to be delivered in American cities and towns prior to the addition of pizza in the 1960s. (See also box P.)

LEFT: This is one of dozens of photos taken by Cathcart to document the highly unusual way in which food was delivered (Cathcart, 1937).

OPPOSITE, TOP TO BOTTOM: As part of the War Relief Association's efforts to educate the uninitiated and to promote Chinatown to European America, Cathcart wrote a note to accompany this photograph. One thing he did not mention was that the restaurant was men-only, which it remained until the 1970s (Cathcart, 1937).

The Tao Yuan Restaurant employees pledged 900 dollars to the
war relief association. Dozens of largers and smaller restaurants
have done substantially the same. This one is favored by
Chinese for its native foods as well as by knowing Americans.
The Chinese restaurants are open at all hours,each has at least
one Tray Man xhxxxwikkxbxingxkixx who carried on his head either
large or small tray of food to Chinese who can not leave their
work or who wish food served in their homes. Thirty Chinese
restaurants are listed in the telephone book.Jackson street
contains the largest number. Practically all Chinese patronize
the restaurants,many for all their meals. Food is good and
not expensive by American comparison. In some native restaurants
a meal of soup,meat course,dessert and drink is offered frxm
for 20 tp 35 cents depending upon the entree. Most popular
dessert is apple pie. Most popular drink is coffee,tea xtilix
ixx remains popular with old generation. More Chinese are
employed in restaurants than in any other industry save the
garment trades.

a7

SYMBOL: This is the Chinese character for prosperity: two old Chinese coins joined together to create wealth. It was a popular symbol for Chinese well-wishing, good luck, prosperity, and good fortune, especially during the New Year's celebration and business openings.

a8

FORTY-NINERS: A reference to Chinese immigrants being among the first to arrive in 1849 as part of the Gold Rush, followed by more than one hundred thousand other people. It was these newcomers who named San Francisco "Big City," or *Dai Fow*, for its importance. A story in Herbert Asbury's *Barbary Coast* tells of Chinese boys and young men sifting the dirt of Portsmouth Square for the lost gold dust from miners buying goods and services. About 10 percent of gold dust was lost to handling, which led to the name "Gold Mountain," as the streets were allegedly paved with gold. However, when the Americans arrived in late '49 and '50, most nonwhites were chased out of the gold fields and their claims jumped. (See also box H.)

Claim am Turon Fluße.

LEFT: This 1850 woodblock depicts the mining technique of pumping water into a sluice box, a universal non-exclusionary process to pan for gold.

a9 **MAH JONGG:** Mah-jongg is a game of skill, luck, and strategy common in Chinese culture, which uses an average of 144 characters and differs slightly depending on the region of China in which it is played. This game of chance was often played in the alleys and side streets of Chinatown, where groups assembled in clubs tied to regional and linguistic familiarity. The game is purportedly related to Confucius and the story of the three virtues. It is still hugely popular and can be heard in the alleys behind private clubs.

b1 **VASE OR URN:** Both decorative and historical, urns and vases have been the center of important and timeless designs in Chinese culture and are admired for their ceremonial significance, simplicity of shape, and aesthetic value. Many have specific functions, like interment, but some are simply for flowers. Grant Avenue was full of vendors selling well-made wares, many of which were the best imported products available nationwide. (See also box a6.)

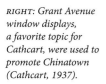

RIGHT: Grant Avenue window displays, a favorite topic for Cathcart, were used to promote Chinatown (Cathcart, 1937).

MODERN SLIT-SKIRT DRESS: This was a new style as of the 1930s and represented the modernization of the Chinese American woman. It showed a natural integration of Western modernity and traditional styles that marked the epitome of sophistication and professionalism for the majority of these middle-class women, who were merchants or had careers in business or services.

RIGHT & FOLLOWING PAGES: While some Chinese American women adopted Western-style dress, others wore clothes that retained symbolically important elements of traditional dress (Cathcart, 1937). • The qipao, a traditional one-piece dress, which has a fitted waist, an upright Mandarin collar, and side slits, was modernized over the years, undergoing variations on its classic features—hemlines rose, sleeves became shorter, the silhouette more form-fitting, and side slits more revealing (Cathcart, 1937–38).

b2

"THE UPPER PART OF SACRAMENTO, WHOLE LENGTH OF DUPONT . . . QUARTER OFTEN CALLED LITTLE CHINA"— ANNALS 1854: This is a quote from the book *The Annals of San Francisco* by Frank Soule, John H. Gihon, and Jim Nisbet. Published in 1854, it was the first book about the newly formed city of San Francisco and its short history and rapid transformation since 1847. This "in the moment" publication captures the attitudes of the day and the prevailing sentiments of both established Californios and newcomer Americans. Acknowledgment of the early Chinese community, regardless of how it was described, was important.

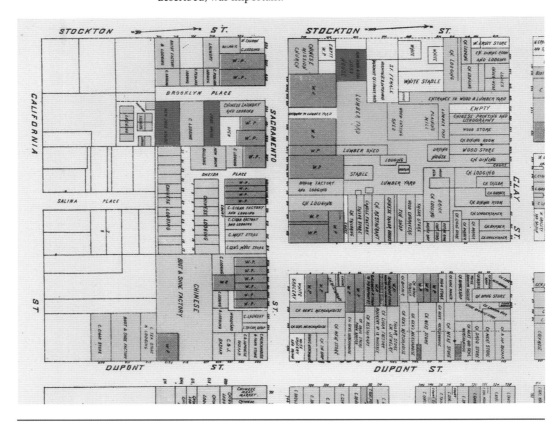

LEFT: This close-up of the 1885 Official Map of Chinatown in San Francisco depicts Chinatown thirty years after its founding, showing that the original area had become brothels of white prostitution and Chinatown had spread out greatly (see also pages 12–13).

b3

WELCOME AT OLD BAZAAR: Probably a reference to a business sign that was actually on Grant Avenue. The old bazaars were the mainstay of Grant Avenue retail culture, selling high-quality goods representative of San Francisco's status as a major West Coast port.

CHI ICON: *Chi* is life energy or the flow of energy—not to be confused with *cha*, or tea, which might make more sense for a tea shop. There were many tea shops on Grant Avenue, and we think Cathcart had tea with clients as a way to get to know them. Although this tea is shown with a figure in allegedly traditional garb, the robe is cut too high, the shoes are wrong for the dress, and the mandarin outfit presented might offend learned Chinese Americans rather than please them.

THE STOCKTON TUNNEL: This tunnel, inaugurated by Mayor James Rolph in 1914, is the transit connection between downtown and the Chinatown–North Beach areas, reflecting the value of the northern neighborhoods to the downtown community, and vice versa, for business.

RIGHT: This 1860s woodblock from a German newspaper depicts a scene from Sacramento Street, looking west, uphill from Kearny Street toward Grant Avenue through the original location of Chinatown.

FOLLOWING PAGES: Tea has played a vital role in China's history since ancient times, dating back almost five thousand years. Originally used for its medicinal properties, tea became popular for everyday leisurely use. As plantations spread throughout China, tea was traded as a highly prized commodity (Cathcart, 1937).

Die Sacramentoſtraße in San Francisco.

b4

DONALDINE CAMERON'S RESCUE MISSION: Founded in 1874 and originally called the Occidental Mission Home for Girls, this building was located at 920 Sacramento Street as a Christian rescue mission for young women and girls who were indentured as slaves or prostitutes. In the 1890s, the mission became successful through the efforts of the eponymic Donaldina Cameron (misspelled in Cathcart's map), who worked with the Chinese immigrant community to eliminate economic and sexual exploitation. Cameron was famous for going into the dens and physically removing victims in the face of danger. Also known as "White Devil," she was threatened by tongs and criminals throughout her entire life of ninety-eight years. In the 1906 earthquake, the building was dynamited to reduce the spread of fire, and the mission, girls, and teachers were all temporarily moved to Oakland. In late 1907, their building was rebuilt on the same site, and all the women returned. In 1942, the name was changed to the Cameron House. The organization has Presbyterian Christian backing and still works on behalf of the Asian and Chinese immigrants within our society.

LEFT: The Cameron House, originally named the Occidental Mission Home for Girls, is still an important fixture in Chinatown. Pictured here circa 1910, the school, which many locals attended, is still used today for programs and services to help the community.

SCH.: This Chinese immersion school building, Jung Wah School, was located at 925 Stockton Street at Sacramento in a segregated city. The attending children were Chinese Americans and were taught the traditional ways of the old country. Founded in 1888 (incorporating an older school established in 1859), the school appears to have still been in the process of being rebuilt at the time Cathcart created his map. It was the property of the Presbyterians and was then transferred to private ownership, perhaps under the banner of the Six Companies. Today, it is the Central Chinese High School at 827–829 Stockton and continues to educate Chinese American students in Chinese culture, language, and math.

SIX COMPANIES: An early cadre of six politically connected families, the organization promoted community and protected ethnic identity. Until there was a Chinese embassy, the Six Companies worked on behalf of the Chinese in America for seventy-five years, representing Chinese Americans in the creation of railroads and reconstruction of Chinatown after the 1906 earthquake and fire, and defending Chinese rights in civil lawsuits in front of the US Supreme Court. The Six Companies also owned the Kong Chow Temple and the Chinese immersion school next door. (See also box Z.)

OPPOSITE, TOP TO BOTTOM: This circa 1903 photo of the officers of the Chinese Six Companies, a benevolent association made up of affluent immigrants, came from Cathcart's personal reference photos. • The Six Companies founded the Chinese War Relief Association to raise funds to aid civilians trapped in China during the Second Sino-Japanese War (Cathcart, 1937).

b5

FONG CHONG OR "LITTLE PETE, DUKE OF VICE" WITH "LO FÄN" AND DOG: "Little Pete" (born Fung Jing Toy) was the infamous gambling king of Chinatown. There is an arrow pointing toward the second story of Waverly Place at the corner of Washington Street, where Little Pete supposedly resided (above the shoe company at 819½ Washington). The other arrow, pointing to the ground floor of the same building at 817 Washington, references the barbershop where Little Pete was killed.

Little Pete came to San Francisco at the age of ten and worked for a shoe company, and then later for the Six Companies. He grew up during the Tong Wars and soon became directly involved. After years of gambling, crime, murder, and typical highbinder (assassin) activity, he became the leader of it all. Little Pete was wanted for $3,000, so he hired a white bodyguard by the name of C.H. Hunter. He hoped to discourage highbinders from going after a white person. Hunter is represented in the figure to the left of Little Pete captioned "Lo Fän," a pejorative meaning "white devil," historically applied to white men. Hunter likely celebrated the word as a projection of his force over his enemies.

A related element in box c5 is "d. 1892," which we believe is a reference to the story of Little Pete's death at the barbershop. Some sources cite his death date as January 1887, others 1897. Cathcart most likely had some reputable sources that he used in his telling of the famous story of Little Pete, confirming his death in 1892, although current research reveals that the date is still in dispute.

BELOW: The building on the left still houses a barbershop, as it did in Little Pete's time. This corner location, with his residence on the second floor, is the site at which he was killed.

BELOW, LEFT TO RIGHT: The Chinese School, which opened in 1859, was renamed the Oriental Public School in 1906 (where children of Asian descent were forced to attend), eventually becoming the Commodore Stockton School in 1924 and finally the Gordon J. Lau Elementary School in 1998. • Because schools and hospitals were not open to Chinese people, the San Francisco Chinese Hospital, the first and only all-Chinese hospital in the United States, was opened in 1925 with money from Chinese Americans. (Cathcart, 1938.)

b6

COM. STOCKTON SCH.: This school was named after Commodore Robert F. Stockton of the American Navy, who commanded troops during the Mexican-American War in 1847. He was the head of operations until he handed control of California over to General Stephen Kearny in compliance with orders from Washington, D.C. It is located at 936 Washington Street and is currently the location of the Commodore Stockton Child Development Center. It is situated across the street from Gordon Lau Elementary School, named after Gordon J. Lau (1941–1998), the first Chinese American elected to the San Francisco Board of Supervisors in 1977.

CHINESE HOSP., 1924: Located at 845 Jackson Street, this hospital was an important medical facility for a previously ignored populace. It had well-trained, multilingual staff and good doctors, often American-trained and/or American-born Chinese. It was paid for by the Chinese community and subsequently supported by the greater medical system. The hospital was torn down in 2015 and reconstructed to be about ten times bigger. Many Chinatown children have been born in this facility.

b7

SLAVE GIRL, BODIE: "Bodie" may be a reference to Bodie, California, now a ghost town and national landmark, which was founded in 1876 as a Gold Rush boomtown with five thousand miners. It was known for having a Chinatown, complete with temples and opium dens, and a red-light district, where a prostitute by the name of Rosa May was famed for being a "hooker with a heart of gold." The woman pictured here is in the traditional costume of a Chinese slave girl. There are local tales of brothel owners buying ten- to sixteen-year-old girls as slaves from cow pens on St. Louis Alley. These children were brought from China and forced into prostitution by the tongs. Some were lured under false pretenses of work or education. This tale is dark, but the icon itself seems rather "glossy," or romanticized, as an emulation of a Suydam drawing of the same from his book, which depicted all aspects of Chinatown positively.

Chinese Slave Girl.

LEFT: This idealized illustration of a Chinese "slave girl" belies the horrific realities young women faced in Chinatown's sex trade.

b8

AN UNIDENTIFIED BLONDE WOMAN WITH A PONY OR DONKEY: For this seemingly incongruous addition, the artist may have been motivated by *horror vacui*, or the aversion to leaving empty space unadorned, a widespread practice with the early cartographers of the sixteenth and seventeenth centuries.

b9

LITTLE MEXICO: Cilantro, cactus, tortillas, and a corn grinder are all the tools necessary for a quality Mexican Californio's meal, celebrating the Hispanic connection to the 800 block of Broadway. This represents the area around Broadway and Stockton-Powell, an homage to the earliest San Franciscans. In 1847, this was the edge of the town of Yerba Buena, with the Juana Briones rancho extending uphill from Vallejo Street. Thereafter, Little Mexico was the residence of the Spanish speakers—San Franciscans whose heritage predates San Francisco. The Californios, who traced their history to Yerba Buena, the Presidio, or the Mission, often observed their masses and christenings at Our Lady of Guadalupe Church. Little Mexico is the predecessor of today's Mission District as a center for Latino culture in San Francisco and was all but destroyed by the disruption from the construction of the Broadway Tunnel.

RIGHT: This view of "Little Mexico," the area where Spanish-speaking residents resided, looks down the 900 block of Broadway Street, across Mason Street (Cathcart, 1939).

c1

MERCHANT OF 1850S: This illustration depicts a traditionally outfitted Chinese man with a queue and hat, curly-toed shoes, and a yoke for the transportation of goods. This merchant represents the first generation of Chinese immigrants to arrive with something more than the clothes on their backs—the first generation of middle-class Chinese Americans. They had some capital and the knowledge and ability to invest and generate more capital through the process of manufacturing or the sale of goods.

LEFT: *These newspaper woodblocks depict the fashion of Chinese Americans in the 1850s and reflect the Western fascination with all things "Oriental" at the time.*

c2

***OLD CHINATOWN* BY GENTHE AND IRWIN:** This book, written in 1908 by German photographer Arnold Genthe and edited by Will Irwin, set the tone of the portrayal of Chinatown, Chinese immigrants, and Chinese Americans for the twentieth century. It was a huge influence on the history of photography at the turn of the century, including the publication of photographic books. Genthe is also significant for his rare capturing of pre-earthquake San Francisco. (See direct illustrative homage to Genthe's work in boxes X and L.) Additionally, the Papa Coppa restaurant was a favorite hangout for these two as well as Cathcart during the 1930s. (See also box e5.)

LEFT: *This photograph of pre-earthquake Sacramento Street in 1903 by Arnold Genthe was published in his 1908 book,* Pictures of Old Chinatown.

GRACE CHURCH '06: This church collapsed in the 1906 earthquake and was rebuilt as Grace Cathedral, located half a block off the map. On this site, Cogswell College was built, starting in 1910, and remained there for seventy years, eventually becoming the Ritz-Carlton Hotel. Cathcart took photos of the new cathedral from 1939 to 1940 while it was still under construction.

RIGHT: Grace Church, destroyed in the 1906 earthquake, was replaced by Grace Cathedral, photographed here while still under construction (Cathcart, 1939).

SING FAT'S BAZAAR: Structures like these were established under the pretense of creating a new Chinatown after the earthquake and fire of 1906 and were the first structures constructed after the disaster. These buildings don't exist in China and are viewed with confusion by most non–San Franciscan Chinese. The builders believed the architecture would draw white people's imagination into a "Chinese" experience.

RIGHT & FAR RIGHT: This trade card, a popular form of advertising during the nineteenth and twentieth centuries, was for the Sing Fat Company, run by a Chinese businessman who imported and exported goods. • The Sing Fat Bazaar, one of the oldest marketplaces in Chinatown, portrays a Western interpretation of Cantonese architectural elements (Cathcart, 1938).

SING FAT CO., INC.
THE FAMOUS ORIENTAL BAZAAR
S.W. CORNER CALIFORNIA ST. AND GRANT AVE.,
CHINATOWN.
SAN FRANCISCO, CALIFORNIA.
BRANCH: 548-550 SOUTH BROADWAY,
LOS ANGELES.
司公發生埠正山金國美

c3

SING CHONG: The Sing Chong Retail Temple's design was similar to that of Sing Fat (see box c2). As a pair, they demarcated the entrance to Chinatown, as there was no "gate" yet at Grant and Bush.

LEFT: *A 1923 business card from one of the most well-known Chinatown bazaars, the Sing Chong Company.*

OPPOSITE: *After the 1906 earthquake, in an effort to avoid being relocated to the outskirts of San Francisco, prominent Chinese citizens had Chinatown rebuilt in a pastiche of classical Chinese architectural styles to create a tourist destination and thereby secure the neighborhood's future. The Sing Chong building was one of the first structures to open (Cathcart, 1938).*

SING CHONG IMPORTING CO.
LEADING CHINESE BAZAAR

DIRECT IMPORTERS
SINCE 1906

Wholesale and Retail
Dealers in
FULL LINE OF ORIENTAL ART GOODS
▽▲▽
MAIL ORDERS PROMPT ATTENTION
601–611 GRANT AVENUE
Cor. California

Telephone CHina 0080   SAN FRANCISCO, CALIFORNIA

SING CHONG COMPANY, INC.
Leading Chinese Bazaar, California and Grant Avenue
San Francisco, Cal.

Confucian Society icon and signage: The Confucian Society was established in 1929 by leaders of the Chinese Constitutionalist Democratic Party (CCDP) for the purpose of uniting the Chinese community in the United States with orthodox Confucianism. As a peripheral organization to the CCDP, the society operated the Kung Gow or Confucian School in San Francisco. The building was located at 888 Brooklyn Alley, but seems to have concluded its business by 1945 and thus closed during Cathcart's research period.

FAR LEFT & LEFT: A lithograph of a romanticized alley scene, by E.H. Suydam. • The Confucian Society as it looked in 1937, at 888 Brooklyn Alley, a one-block street (Cathcart, 1937).

Mansion House Pl.: Mansion House Place was the alcove entryway to the Parisian Mansion Brothel, a secured area for viewing the "merchandise" without fully entering the building or having to pay.

Tong war icons and hatchet man: This illustration depicts a pursued tong member running from a hatchet man down Waverly Place, likely during the Tong Wars of the 1880s. "Highbinders," or members of any Chinese American society involved in criminal activities (such as hired killings or blackmail), were hired by each tong to represent them in battle and to enforce the family business. In part because this was beyond the control of law enforcement authorities of the time, this was documented in the newspapers and followed with interest nationwide. Herbert Asbury writes of these wars in great detail in his book, *The Barbary Coast*. Sometime between 1887 and 1888, after several highly visible clashes on Waverly Place resulted in deaths, a peace was brokered. Later, organizations like the Peace Society were formed, and efforts were more greatly focused. Nonetheless, these peaceful periods were generally short-lived, and clashes over lovers, dogs, soup recipes, theater seats, and many other perceived slights continued well into the 1930s.

LEFT & BELOW: Illustrations of highbinders, or professional killers, and the tools of their trade, as shown in an 1880 newspaper.

OPPOSITE: The alleyways of Chinatown, depicted here in a nineteenth-century German newspaper, were where most of the vice occurred.

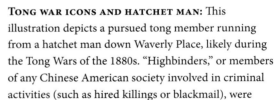

c4

PLAYGROUND: This playground, which included tennis courts, was a sacred place in the densely populated urban area. A cornerstone of childhood in Chinatown, it was a safe space and serves the same role today as it did when it was built. However, the recreational building has been rebuilt, and there are no longer slides. It was illustrated in Dobie and Suydam's 1936 book, *San Francisco's Chinatown*, and is explored by Gordon Chin in his video, "Saving Chinese Playground," which is available on YouTube.

LEFT, TOP TO BOTTOM: The half-acre playground, which was built in 1927, was for many years the only outdoor space in all of Chinatown for locals to utilize. By 1935, tennis had become a popular pastime in San Francisco. • Children could often be seen enjoying the slides. • This vantage point from the rooftop of the YMCA across the street, of which Mrs. B.S. Fong was the director, shows the playground from above. (Cathcart, 1937.)

RIGHT: Tongs were powerful organized crime networks, but were also some of the few resources immigrants could turn to in difficult times. Pictured here is the Bing Kong Tong building (Cathcart, 1939).

BING KONG TONG: This was the family building of the Bing Kong Tong, which was one of the more powerful tongs in Chinatown in the early twentieth century. They were at the center of many tong conflicts of the nineteenth century.

PAGODA: Pagoda Alley was also known as Hang Ah Alley, or Perfumers Alley, named for the sale of fragrances by a German dealer doing business in Chinatown in the 1870s. It maintains the mystique of narrow "Chinatown alleyways" even today. Lining the playground on the uphill side with a good view of the tennis courts, it was a popular place for Cathcart to document the activities of the community. It also had market stalls for the sale of goods in his time.

RIGHT: An automobile is parked on Hang Ah Alley, which runs alongside the tennis courts of Chinatown's playground (Cathcart, 1937).

YOUNG CHINA: This was a Chinese-language newspaper business on the corner of Clay and Stockton, covering news from China and communities of Chinese people around the world. *Young China* is one of several important representations of the value of freedom of speech to the Chinese and Chinese American communities.

RIGHT & FAR RIGHT: Men assemble to read the day's news from the Young China *posted in the window (Cathcart, 1937).*

WONG FAM.: The Wong family building was the center of Wong family activity, located at Waverly Place. During Cathcart's mapmaking work, the bottom floor was used for retail and inhabited by a Wong family member, while the upper floors contained meeting rooms and a temple.

WAVERLY PL. (PIKE): Pike Alley, which was home to many of the family buildings and associations, was more often known as Waverly Place. The name "Pike" has disappeared from common use.

LEFT: This picture of the Wong family building was likely used for reference on Cathcart's map (Cathcart, 1937).

HANG FAR LOW: Built during the 1880s, this two-story restaurant was part of Look Tin Eli's efforts to promote a non-Chinese architect designing and reconstructing the razed Chinatown community after the 1906 earthquake and fire. The clever name was not wasted on the tourists, and locals and owners were well aware of the not-so-subtle innuendo. Food and service were considered very good, and the decor was comprised of rosewood panels, inlaid with mother-of-pearl and jade, as well as table displays and private booths. It was a popular gathering spot for both old-timers and modern Chinatown residents, and was the setting for many important meetings in the 1930s. It was also a favorite hangout of Cathcart and his friends.

LEFT: This view up the 700 block of Grant Avenue shows Iwata on the corner, with Hang Far Low, a restaurant famous for its private booths, halfway up the block (Cathcart, 1937).

RIGHT: Cathcart and his friends spent a fair amount of time at Hang Far Low, pictured here in various scenes, because it was known for its friendly atmosphere and likely suited their palate and budget (Cathcart, 1937).

AN OLD PODII: This refers to an unspoken rule that, in the event that a property owner should treat his or her tenants unfairly, the building would not be rented to any other person until the wronged tenants had been compensated. On this map, it refers to a specific building on the corner of Grant and Clay. The phrasing is a reference to Dobie's *Chinatown*, in which he quotes Tom Irwin's contemporary article in the *Chronicle*: "The podii guaranteed an evicted tenant against unscrupulous practices, permitted him to place an indemnity on vacated property. Such property could not be rented until the indemnity was satisfied. Should any Chinese rent it, he would inevitably go broke . . ." Cathcart's photos of this corner show it with a "to lease" sign in every shot for years.

RIGHT: This view up Grant Avenue shows the view from Clay Street south, with the Old Podii building in the foreground (Cathcart, 1937).

c5

St. Mary's Sch.: A Catholic elementary school on Clay, between Stockton and Spofford Alley, with administration quarters and a courtyard for recess. All of these schools were segregated and were for Chinese children only, and this one was supported by Catholic charities. A building still stands in this location today with a cross on top, but doesn't function as a school.

Lee: The Lee building was the location of the Lee Lung Si Tong Association, at 109 Waverly Place, next to Sun Lee Carpenters, site of the oldest existing private family temple in the United States.

LEFT: The Lee Lung Si Tong Association, with a lookout above and the family business below, is still in operation today (Cathcart, 1938).

Tin How Temple: Founded at 125 Waverly Place in 1852, it was the first Taoist temple in San Francisco and still operates today, making it one of the oldest in the United States. It is dedicated to the worship of the sea goddess Mazu (Tian Hou), also known as Tin How in Cantonese. (See also box S.)

RIGHT: Tin How Temple's altar, which miraculously survived the 1906 earthquake and fire, looks much the same here as it did during the time of the Gold Rush (Cathcart, 1938).

Hop Sing: The Hop Sing Tong building was established at 137 Waverly Place in 1875. At the time of this map's creation, it was most likely another important contributing family association. It had a history of violence, including an incident in 1916 during which five Hop Sing members were involved in taking a Suey Sing member's seat in a theater, and the Suey Sing member subsequently shot them. This killing started another Tong War, which ran for a year.

RIGHT & FAR RIGHT: These pictures show the Tin How and the Hop Sing buildings the day after a political event was held in the area, as evidenced by the trash in the gutters, which was an unusual occurrence at that time (Cathcart, 1943).

Peace Soc.: The Peace Society was established at 160 Waverly Place in 1913 to mediate between rival tongs, settling disputes and creating a neutral space within Chinatown to discuss "peace." This was often aimed at balancing the allocation of money made from gambling and prostitution. Tong battles with hatchet men of the 1880s continued into the 1930s, which explains the inclusion of so much material on this map related to the balance of power in Chinatown.

Ghee Kung Tong: Also known as the Chinese Freemasons Society since 1920, the Ghee Kung Tong building was located at 36 Spofford Alley. A business association focused on the building trades, it spoke on behalf of Chinese builders in San Francisco in the 1930s. It also helped establish standards for hiring, wages, payment, and access to goods. Perhaps its most significant contribution was housing and protecting Sun Yat-sen, who lived in San Francisco for ten years in exile under threat of death from the Qing.

LEFT: *The Ghee Kung Tong, a Chinese fraternal association also referred to as the Chinese Freemasons, was founded in the Gold Rush days to help Chinese immigrants. Sun Yat-sen, known as the father of modern China, hid out at the headquarters of the Chinese Freemasons at 36 Spofford Alley while he was being pursued by agents of the Qing dynasty (Cathcart, 1938).*

LOUIE F. K. FAM.: The Louie Fong Kwong Family Association building was located at the corner of Clay and Dupont, across the street from the old podii. Much of Cathcart's life and documentation radiates out from this corner, which by no coincidence is situated at the center of the map. B.S. Fong was chairman of the Louie Fong Kwong association at this time.

RIGHT: This is the Louie Fong Kwong Family Association building. The Chinese family associations formed in the 1800s to help new immigrants were based on their last names, which signify their home villages in China (Cathcart, 1938).

c6

***Chinese Digest*, also known as *Ching Wah Lee*:** Headquartered at 9 Cameron Place, this newspaper was an important voice for Chinese Americans and Chinese news from abroad. The *Chinese Digest* was a strong supporter of Sun Yat-sen, the Chinese war relief efforts (for the Second Sino-Japanese War), and the repeal of the Exclusion Act. (See also *Young China*, box c4; and *Chung Sai Yat Po*, box d4.)

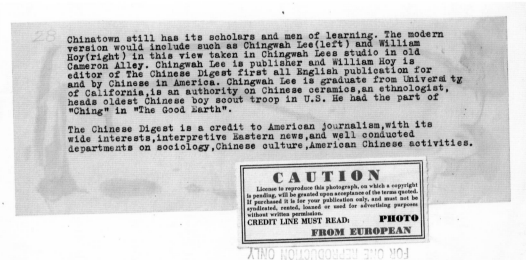

LEFT & BELOW: The Chinese Digest, according to Cathcart's description placed on the back of his photograph, was the "first all-English publication for and by Chinese in America." Other images show the office, inside and out, as well as the editors (Cathcart, 1938).

OPIUM PIPE ICON: This is a reference to the opium dens on Ross Alley, also known as Stout's Alley. It was also marked on the 1885 Chinatown map created by San Francisco's city government. This was generally looked down upon by the white population, yet also became a destination for curious tourists to view the opium resorts and their clientele, who were generally passed out. (See also box c8.)

RIGHT: An opium primer was published in Frank Leslie's Weekly *in the 1870s, telling readers where it comes from, how it is ingested, and the results of partaking.*

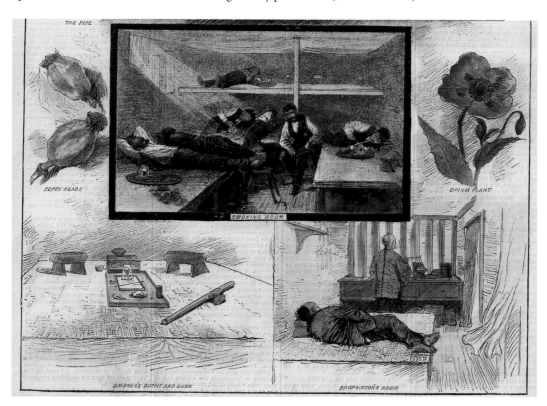

PAWNSHOP: Located at 878 Washington Street, Yick Lung may have been the only pawnshop in Chinatown, dealing in gold, tokens, coins, and precious metals. This was also a place where one could buy musical instruments (see also boxes K and Y). We think Cathcart pawned his camera here once or twice. At the time, purchases were restricted through racist pawnbroker laws, which were specifically set up to restrict Jews and Chinese. These laws required excessive details and records for even the simplest of transactions of precious metals, stones, and fine art.

RIGHT: Yick Lung, a pawnshop in Chinatown, eventually closed its doors in 1969. Pawnshops played a significant role in ancient China, as they were a major source of loans. In Chinatown in the 1930s, however, it was considered degrading to pawn anything (Cathcart, 1943).

ROSS (STOUT'S) ALLEY: This was a street known for gambling, where basement-level cribs had escape passages between locations to avoid raids by law enforcement authorities. The sidewalks in much of San Francisco's Chinatown and North Beach are hollow to the street, meaning there is often open space underneath the sidewalk for the merchant or property owner to use. These areas were often connected to one another; the ability to move unrestricted always has value in a culture restrained at every turn. The California Historical Society issue of Cathcart's map shows these alleyways connecting to numerous underground passageways (as implied on this map at box d3). Despite most of these tunnels being destroyed in the 1906 earthquake and fire, many of these connected sidewalks still exist today.

FAR LEFT & LEFT: Ross Alley, named after a pioneer merchant who built a house there in 1849, was a notorious one-block alley in the heart of Chinatown once noted for gambling, opium, brothels, and tong conflicts. • This engraving from an 1885 German newspaper depicts basement access to a building. There were also underground tunnels connecting the buildings of Chinatown, which were destroyed in the 1906 earthquake and fire.

CHAN FAM.: The Chan family built this building for business at 826–830 Washington Street in 1901, represented at the end of Waverly on Washington. It was rebuilt in 1964 to modernize and update the property.

LEFT: Waverly Place is shown here in the early morning, looking north toward the Chan family building (Cathcart, 1937).

1ST CHINESE LAUNDRY, '51: San Francisco's first Chinese laundry was established in 1851. Laundry was an essential business, as all people needed it and it had no regulation. It cost about $75–100 to start one, as the basic equipment required was a tub, a trough with drainage, and laundry soap. Famous San Francisco laundries include the Chinese laundry at the Washerwoman's Lagoon in Cow Hollow from 1851 until 1870. It was the busiest laundry, with a two-month waiting list for the return of one's clothing in 1853; this wait time shrank as more laundries came into existence. The capital made from laundries has created a lot of wealth over time, and the quality associated with Chinese laundries has been a long-standing point of pride.

RIGHT: The garment industry was Chinatown's largest employer in the 1930s, but the conditions were deplorable and wages were low. In response, the International Ladies' Garment Workers' Union (ILGWU) began organizing in Chinatown to make sure the work was done in union shops and established the Chinese Ladies' Garment Workers' Union (Cathcart, 1938).

OLD BULLETIN BOARD: The tongs posted notices here announcing who had a price on their head, as well as prostitute auctions, lottery winners, "job" postings, general tong business communication, and open declarations between tongs.

RIGHT: The tongs communicated with each other, including declaring war, by bulletins posted on walls (Cathcart, 1938).

SALVATION ARMY: In addition to those of the Cameron House, some other Christians were also interested in creating better conditions for Chinatown, and this manifested through the Salvation Army. Events, fundraisers, clothing drives, and representation were provided, with most staff (such as nuns and reverends) still wearing habits of their faith in public.

SUEY SING TONG: The Suey Sing Tong building was founded at 915 Grant Avenue in 1867. Some members of the Suey Sing were famous participants of the April 1875 battle with the Kwong Duck Tong on Waverly Place. Essentially, it was a war over a woman called "the Golden Peach." This lovely prostitute was involved in a love triangle with an admiring member from each group. In the end, after a great ten-minute battle that left three dead and twelve or more wounded, a peace was brokered with apologies and payments transpiring; the Peach married one of the two men. On another occasion in 1916, a member of the Suey Sing Tong shot five Hop Sing members when his seat was taken in a theater, which started another Tong War.

LEFT & BELOW: These images show a number of family organizations and tongs—the word tong *literally translates into "hall"—along the 900 block of Grant Avenue, one of the oldest streets in Chinatown (Cathcart, 1939).*

ST. LOUIS AL.: St. Louis Alley was the site of slave auctions and tong business, documented (but romanticized and cleaned up) by E.H. Suydam and Arnold Genthe. This is a place where tongs sold young women and girls into slavery. The women were bought or kidnapped in China and transported to San Francisco, where they were sold into a life of terminal servitude. Life expectancy was three years for these ten- to sixteen-year-old children. (See also box b7.)

OPPOSITE: A Suydam illustration of the infamous St. Louis Alley, where young girls were sold to brothel owners in slave auctions.

St. Louis Alley.

(From Jackson Street, looking North.)

c7

ALLEYWAYS: Pontiac, Duncombe, and Sullivan (today named Jason) Alleys. Newspaper articles of the time regard alleyways as places to be approached with caution, due to pimps lying in wait for customers. The 1885 map reveals housed concentrations of Chinese and white prostitution at this site.

BELOW & BOTTOM: The maze of alleyways in Chinatown was the result of the need to maximize space by a community relegated to a six-block area (Cathcart, 1938). • Promotional material for the Mandarin (Cathcart, 1937).

A LOOK-OUT: Lookouts like this waited on the street to inform others of the arrival of the authorities or competing interests to ensure that whatever activities taking place would not be interfered with. Historically, gambling, opium "resorts," and brothels employed lookouts. The fact that this man is wearing a bowler hat and a queue indicates that he is a pre-1930s Chinese American.

HOW WONG TEMPLE: Our research has not turned up any information on this temple with regard to its owners, deity, or family served. However, Cathcart did take a photo of it located at the center of a block lost to public housing development around the time of the map. The temple no longer exists.

MANDARIN TH.: The Mandarin Theatre was built at 1021 Grant Avenue in 1925. It was a traditional Chinese theater employing live actors, depicting traditional stories and operatic tales with elaborate costumes and sets. The Mandarin was one of two active Chinese theaters in San Francisco, the other being the Great China Theater. The 1920s and 1930s constituted the golden age of Chinese opera in the United States, with female performers leading the charge (as opposed to the male-dominated opera theaters in China at the time). The Mandarin continued to operate until 1949, when it was changed into a movie theater, which remained until 1986. In 1948, Orson Welles used the buildings as his set for his film *The Lady from Shanghai.*

OPPOSITE, CLOCKWISE FROM TOP: The Mandarin Theatre, built in 1925, was a venue for live opera before it eventually became a movie theater (Cathcart, 1939). • Prosperous Chinese theaters enthralled audiences with Cantonese opera, where elaborately costumed Asian performing troupes took center stage (Cathcart, 1939). • The Mandarin Theatre entryway is pictured here decorated with posters depicting current and previous productions (Cathcart, 1937).

5A-H1070

c8

FUN FOR HOODLUMS: Cutting off queues was aggressively racist harassment by teenage boys, written about in periodicals in the 1850s to 1880s. It was part of the dehumanizing campaign supported through media and not halted by police.

PIPE OF DREAMS: This is a reference to historical opium use, as shown on the 1885 map. Opium use and gambling were not illegal in the nineteenth century, and fascinated Westerners based on the news coverage.

LEFT & BELOW: Considered treason to cut one's queue, keeping it intact was the only way to return safely to China. This 1887 German illustration, whose title translates to "unpopular population," highlights the offense. • Chinese immigrants brought opium with them, and opium dens were prevalent in Chinatown, as illustrated here in an 1887 newspaper.

c9

"W. Fong": An unidentified photographer at Columbus and Broadway.

LEFT: While Arnold Genthe would often hide his camera to get a candid shot, street photographers would ideally become neutral bystanders in order to depict but not influence everyday life (Cathcart, 1948).

d1

POODLE DOG '69–'98: Established in 1849 at Bush and Grant, Le Poulet D'or—commonly known as the Poodle Dog—was one of San Francisco's first and most famous French restaurants. The origin of the nickname remains obscure. One story is that a couple of Frenchmen, Messrs. Peguillan and Langsman, opened the restaurant. Mme. Peguillan owned a small, white poodle. Both the dog and the wife were rarities in young San Francisco, drawing as much attention to the restaurant as its cuisine. The poodle, called Ami, assumed the position of host and greeted the customers, causing some to consider Ami the proprietor and unofficially name the restaurant after the dog. The restaurant moved to the Grant and Bush Street location in 1868, officially taking on the Old Poodle Dog name. Despite the death of its eponymic canine early on, it remained a hugely popular dining establishment, known for its lavish four-course meals with all the trimmings, until it closed in 1898.

ABOVE RIGHT & RIGHT: While purebreds like Le Poulet D'or's poodle (if the story of the origin of the restaurant's name holds true) would have been exempt from being impounded at the turn of the twentieth century, mixed-breed dogs, such as the one pictured here, were in danger. • This 1869 playbill from the wildly popular California Theatre is for the thirty-ninth week of its first year.

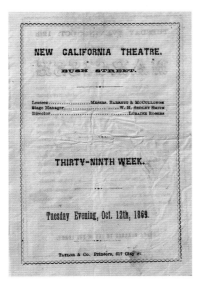

CAL. TH. '69: The California Theatre was built in 1869 by William Ralston, founder of the Bank of California, at 414 Bush Street (now 430–440). The theater cost $250,000 and opened on January 18, 1869. It cleared $100,000 in its first year and was an immediate success. It was intended as a worthy venue for Ralston's favorite actors, John McCullough and Lawrence Barrett. Other acting notables performed there, including Edwin Booth, Lotta Crabtree, and Hobart Bosworth. It also functioned as an opera house and hosted singers Inez Fabbri and Nellie Melba. The theater succeeded financially until the mid-1870s, when the Bank of California failed and Ralston drowned in the San Francisco Bay near North Beach. The theater was torn down and rebuilt in 1889, only to be destroyed by the 1906 earthquake and fire. A historical marker is laid at 430 Bush Street to commemorate the location. It is also the first site in the western United States to have modern stage lighting (derived from mining technology) based on calcium oxide, also known as "limelight."

BENNY BUFANO, HIS SUN, HIS FRIEND: This is a reference to the Sun Yat-sen statue in St. Mary's Square (see box d2), created by Beniamino Bufano, a well-known San Francisco–based Italian American sculptor. He was a friend of Sun, who wrote the Constitution of the Republic of China (1912–1949) while exiled in San Francisco. This statue was dedicated with an unveiling to support positive Sino-American relations, which shaped the conversation surrounding the repeal of the Chinese Exclusion Act. Bufano also did work for the Panama–Pacific International Exposition of 1915 and the Golden Gate International Exposition of 1939, under contract with the Works Progress Administration. His works are all over San Francisco, with his St. Francis of Assisi work being the most well known. Beneath Bufano's head is a symbol, which seems to be Cathcart's attempt at a Chinese character meaning "longevity," perhaps through fame or notoriety. We see this design elsewhere on the map, above "Ah Chic" (see box d7) and to the right of Emperor Norton (see box e4). It looks most like a Chinese design element, of which so many have been appropriated by other cultures.

LEFT: Sun Yat-sen, whose anti-imperialist activism helped overthrow the feudal Qing dynasty in 1912, lived in exile in San Francisco. Pacifist Bufano, who had met Sun Yat-sen in China in 1920, received the commission from Chinatown business leaders to erect a statue in his honor (Cathcart, 1939).

ST. MARY'S PARK:
d2 St. Mary's Square (not "park") and the Bufano statue of Sun Yat-sen still exist, but construction of St. Mary's Square Garage underneath the park eliminated the severe slope of the park, which was a center for neighborhood activities, including memorial services and public speaking events.

LEFT & BELOW: A man sleeps it off in St. Mary's Square, six years after the repeal of prohibition (Cathcart, 1939).
• Cathcart, who was hired to document Chinatown events, took this shot of a ceremony in St. Mary's Square (Cathcart, 1938).

Sun Yat-sen: Sun Yat-sen, perhaps the most important Chinese person ever to have lived in San Francisco, was commemorated by Benny Bufano's 1937 statue. After Sun Yat-sen's attempt to overthrow the Qing dynasty failed in 1895, he fled to America, pursued by agents of the Chinese government. The Ghee Kung Tong protected, housed, and raised money for Sun during his time in San Francisco until he returned to China in 1911. There, Sun defeated the Qing and helped establish the first Republic of China. Western democracies considered the constitution of the Chinese Republic to be an ideological milestone. This allowed the United States government to gradually promote and further support friendlier political dialog with China, which had been villainized, marginalized, and dehumanized during the nineteenth century. Sun's revolutionary democratic ideas and his relationship with the United States through San Francisco were very important to Chinese Americans of this period.

RIGHT: Bufano, who created the statue of Sun Yat-sen, a revered statesman who fought against imperialist aggression, claimed that his art should be "big enough to belong to everybody, too big for anyone to put in his pocket and call his own" (Cathcart, 1938).

KONG CHOW TEMPLE: Originally built at 520 Pine Street in 1875, it was once the largest and most well-known temple in San Francisco. This temple was founded in 1849 as a family clan temple for five groups and dedicated to Guan Di. It burned to the ground in the 1906 earthquake and fire before being rebuilt, and it remained there until its relocation to Stockton Street in 1977. The three-story structure with a pagoda top made of tile was demolished to make way for the St. Mary's Square Garage and the Bank of Hong Kong building. The site was never built upon, despite the building being demolished in 1977, and it sat undeveloped until 2016, close to forty years.

LEFT: The Kong Chow Temple, illustrated here in a German newspaper from 1875, was renamed the Kong Chow Clan Association in 1854, to put the focus on its social endeavors on behalf of the community.

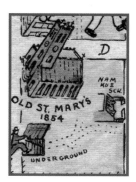

d3

OLD ST. MARY'S 1854: Old St. Mary's Cathedral, constructed in 1854 at 660 California Street, was designed by Thomas England and William Craine and built with "clinker" brick from Connecticut and granite from China. It was built to convey Catholicism to the Chinese in San Francisco and is the oldest cathedral in California. Originally designed with a spire, which was never constructed, it provides a backdrop for many of Cathcart's Grant Avenue photographs. It survived a history of fires and earthquakes and still stands today, in use by Catholic Chinese Americans.

RIGHT, CLOCKWISE FROM TOP: This photograph shows the view from the Russ Building of Old St. Mary's Cathedral, the Kong Chow Temple, and St. Mary's Square (Cathcart, 1938). • This representation of St. Mary's Cathedral, presented in an Annals of San Francisco *from 1855, shows the church with a spire, which never was built. • A Chinese funeral procession files out from Old St. Mary's Cathedral in 1938. Buddhism and Protestant Christianity have been the two most-represented religious denominations amongst the Chinese population throughout Chinatown's history, and St. Mary's remains the only Catholic Chinese church in San Francisco. • St. Mary's Cathedral is nestled close to a Canton bazaar along Grant Avenue (Cathcart, 1938).*

1876: This is the year the California Street Railroad Company (later known as "cable cars") was established and tracks were placed in the middle of the street. Each street car line played a role in the development of Nob Hill and other neighborhoods. Before mechanized transport, only poor people lived on the hills because they had to haul everything up by hand. Flat land was the dominion of the wealthy, until it became fashionable to live on the hill and have a machine carry them to the top.

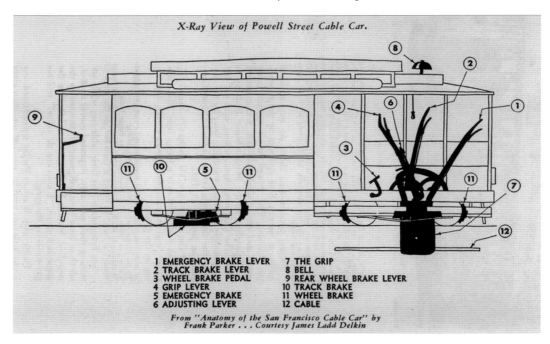

LEFT: This illustration depicting the inner workings of the Powell Street cable car is from the 1946 book Anatomy of the San Francisco Cable Car *and describes exactly how the cars work.*

UNDERGROUND: This icon marks an entrance to the underground tunnel system. Our research has not been able to determine when it was built, but we assume it was prior to the 1906 earthquake. According to a copy of the map housed at the California Historical Society, Cathcart drew numerous tunnels at various locations all over Chinatown, with several running from Pacific Avenue over to the opium resorts and alleys.

NAM KUE SCH.: The Nam Kue School is a Hong Kong–style Chinese school teaching traditional art, culture, language, and mathematics, still in operation today. At the time of this map's creation, it was a church-run, Chinese-only segregated school within Chinatown, providing a decent, albeit strict, education. It was located at 749 (now renumbered 755) Sacramento Street.

BELOW: Chinese schools such as the Nam Kue School were started to keep young Chinese Americans in touch with their Chinese culture, history, and language.

d4

DR. POON CHEW: This refers to Dr. Ng Poon Chew (1866–1931), the creator and editor-in-chief of *Chung Sai Yat Po* newspaper. He immigrated to the United States in 1881 at the age of fifteen, worked as a houseboy on the San Francisco peninsula, and studied English. He became a Presbyterian minister by 1894 and was placed in charge of the Chinese Presbyterian mission in Los Angeles. This was the start of a career focused on righting the inequity of European American laws towards Chinese and China, in which he began to work with the Qing and the Chinese republic governments. He became a vocal political advocate for Chinese Americans, working alongside the Six Companies to lobby the US government to eliminate the Chinese Exclusion Act, which was finally repealed in 1943.

CHUNG SAI YAT PO: This was Ng Poon Chew's newspaper, established in San Francisco in 1900. Also known as *Chinese Western Daily* and *China West Daily*, it was the first Chinese-language newspaper published outside of China. The newspaper was a major supporter of Sun Yat-sen, whose ideas were eminently important to the conversation regarding the political activities of the time. For forty-five years, *Chung Sai Yat Po* was integral in communicating the objections and legal arguments that led to the repeal of the Chinese Exclusion Act. The newspaper ran until 1951.

BELOW: Chung Sai Yat Po, shown here in 1939, was the longest-running Chinese-language daily newspaper until it closed in 1951. The paper encouraged assimilation, trying to bridge the gap between the Chinese and American communities (Cathcart, 1939).

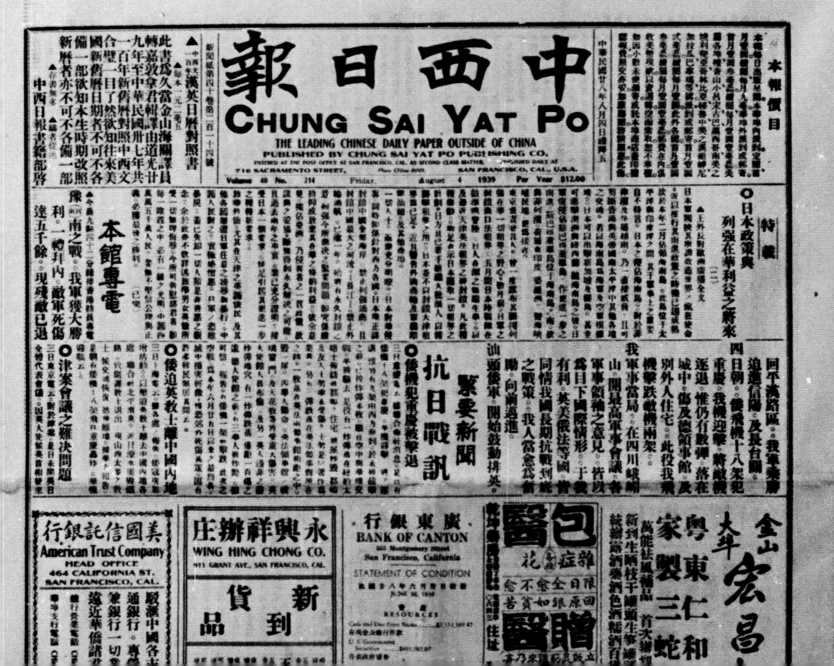

MANSION HOUSE: This was the Parisian Mansion Brothel at 742–746 Commercial Street, one of the most famous of the dozens of brothels along this block as of 1907. It was closed by legislation in 1913, along with most Barbary Coast venues.

HIP SING TONG: The Hip Sing Tong's headquarters were at 761 Clay Street. This was another association embroiled in the Tong Wars. In 1898, a fight over a cat led to a war between the Bing Kong Tong and the Hip Sing Tong.

WALK IN

Mme. Lazarinne & Ladies

730 Commercial Street

Bet. Kearny and Dupont

LEFT: A rare 1903 business card for Madame Lazarinne's, a brothel a few doors down from 730 Commercial Street. During the Gold Rush, women flocked to San Francisco to work in the saloons, gambling halls, and brothels, taking advantage of the scarcity of females.

P.O.: This refers to the first post office in San Francisco, established in 1848 as the only building on Clay Street, which was still a dirt road. The post office was a symbol of civilization and, for the Chinese living in Chinatown, their only contact with that world. Chinatown grew up around this and expanded to twelve square blocks in the middle of town by the time of the 1885 map. Its population also grew from a few dozen in 1848 to "15,180 bunks" with an expectation of a minimum of two persons per bunk. But "women and children also seem[ed] to be stowed away in every available nook and corner without reference to any special accommodation being provided for them," as stated in the *Report of the Special Committee*, which produced the 1885 map. This suggests a minimum population of 30,360, with as much as 50 to 65 percent more than that in reality.

LEFT: Before residential delivery became a permanent service in 1902, customers had to pick up their mail at the post office. This 1855 illustration from The Annals of San Francisco *depicts the post office, with "a faithful representation of the crowds daily applying at that office for letters and newspapers."*

The Post Office, corner of Pike and Clay streets.

d5

OLD THEATRE: This theater may have been "old" even by the time of this map, and likely shut down in the 1930s.

TEL. BLD.: This is the Chinese Telephone Exchange Building, located at 750 Washington Street (modernized and moved to 743 after 1896). Important for development of cultural continuity, the service brought ease of communication, translation skills, internal security of dialog, spatial knowledge of Chinatown, and strong cultural identity. All were greatly supported by this building and its functions, starting very early in the history of the telephone. (See also box J.)

RIGHT: To make a call in the early days of telephone technology, one called up an exchange whose switchboard operators would patch them through to the other party. One of the most famous telephone switchboards was the Chinese Telephone Exchange, which had an all-female workforce after the 1906 earthquake and fire (Cathcart, 1938).

BRENHAM PLACE: This is a street at the top of Portsmouth Square, named after Charles James Brenham (1817–1876), twice the mayor of early San Francisco and known for facing off against vigilante crowds aiming to lynch criminals. Ironically, the site of the first lynching in San Francisco—in 1851, by the first San Francisco Committee of Vigilance—was on this street corner with Clay.

LEFT: This Sarony & Major lithographic view of Portsmouth Square in 1849 shows the El Dorado Saloon, Parker House hotel, and a harbor full of empty ships, beached and rotting in the cove, as their crews had taken off in search of gold.

'97: This date refers to an unknown event.

FAW YUEN: *Faw Yuen* (meaning "flower garden") was an old term for Portsmouth Square, which Cathcart may have heard from older Chinese, but it was not in use during the time this map was made. The square provided a gathering place and was surrounded by mercantile services. It originated as a garden for San Francisco pioneer Jacob P. Leese, and then became the town square of Yerba Buena around 1835. The square was renamed after the USS *Portsmouth*, whose captain and first lieutenant claimed San Francisco, and by extension California, for the United States in July 1846 by raising the American flag at the Mexican customhouse. Portsmouth Square was also the site of San Francisco's first city hall, physically connected to no fewer than three saloons. This site was the cultural crossroads of all aspiring San Franciscans for the first fifty years.

LEFT: Portsmouth Square is a one-block park located on the site of the Grand Plaza, which was the first public square and was established in the nineteenth century when San Francisco was known as Yerba Buena (Cathcart, 1943).

BELOW, TOP TO BOTTOM: An 1880s German newspaper illustrates a cable car from the Clay Street Hill Railroad Company. • *The Clay Street line, shown here in 1873, traveled up a 16 percent grade.*

1873: This was the founding year of the world's first cable car company, the Clay Street Hill Railroad Company. It was founded by cable manufacturer and Rincon Hill resident Andrew Smith Hallidie, who introduced wire rope to California. The railroad started at the foot of Clay Street Hill, in front of City Hall. Hallidie is regarded by many as the father of San Francisco's first practical cable car system. Mechanized help was revolutionary, and in the nineteenth century, engineers were considered heroes. From 1880 until his death in 1900, Hallidie was greatly involved with the San Francisco Mechanics' Institute, founded in 1854, and promoted the entrepreneurs and original thinkers of the time. (Cathcart was also a member of the Institute.)

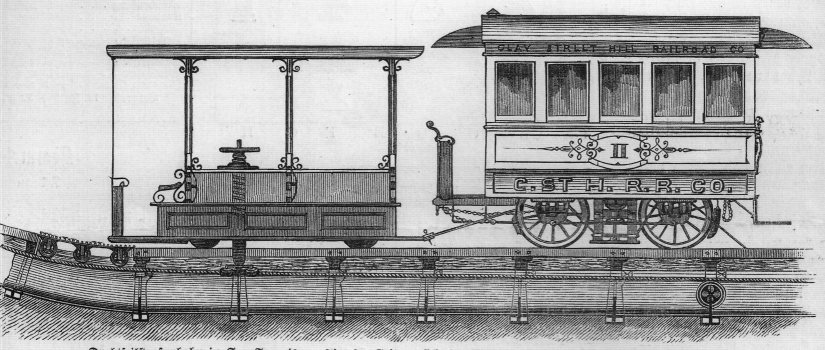

Drahtseilstraßenbahn in San Francisco. Fig. 2. Seitenansicht der Wagen und Längenschnitt durch die Röhre.

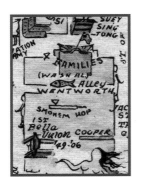

d6

4 Families: The Four Families building on Grant Avenue was another Great Family building. In 1876, the four families—Lew, Quan, Jung, and Chew—built a temple inspired by a seventeenth-century temple in China, which was the center of these families' activities by 1895. Two organizations had the "four families" moniker: the Lung Kong Association and the Mu Tin Association, which later became the Ming Yee Association. The building was built in 1924 as part of these organizational centers, housing mainly Ming Yee Association members and business activities. The Ming Yee were part of the protectionist wing, righting wrongs against their members and maintaining tong agendas.

BELOW & BOTTOM: The Four Families building, halfway down Grant in this shot, was established when the descendants of the families migrated to North America in the late nineteenth century (Cathcart, 1939). • The Kuo Wah Cafe was located on the ground floor of the Four Families building.

Wash. Alley: Washington Alley was the original name of Wentworth Alley, which ran for one block to cross Jackson Street, then, after a slight dogleg, changed back to Bartlett, making its name Washington Bartlett for these two blocks. This was city surveyor William Eddy's nod to San Francisco's first duly elected American alcade.

WENTWORTH PLACE: Wentworth Place was originally identified as Washington Place on Eddy's official 1849 map of San Francisco, and was variously titled "Place" or "Alley" or "Lane" until it was officially named Wentworth Place in the 1909 ordinance. The origin of the name "Wentworth" has not been identified. The fish icon refers to the fact that this alleyway used to be informally called Fish Alley because of the many fish vendors there, according to historian Phil Buscovich.

RIGHT: Lithographers Britton and Rey, who had a company located adjacent to Chinatown at 525 Commercial Street, produced a series of postcards on Chinatown at the turn of the twentieth century, romanticizing and highlighting its exotic traits.

An Alley in Chinatown—Characteristic Scene of many of the small Thoroughfares in this Section of San Francisco

SMOKEM HOP: This opium pipe is stylized but otherwise nondescript; we assume this was an opium den of note. The spelling could be a racist depiction of a Chinese accent.

1ST BELLA UNION, '49–'06: Established at 810 Washington during the Gold Rush, this was the first and most famous gambling hall turned burlesque hall in San Francisco, and is one of the more popular and politically significant saloons in the city's history. It was famous for featuring the entertainers Big Bertha and Oofty Goofty, among others. The business survived here until the 1906 earthquake and fire, then moved to 557 Pacific Avenue. (See also box e7.)

BELOW: This 1851 illustration of Portsmouth Square, the city's first public square, when San Francisco was still Yerba Buena, shows the Bella Union across the plaza.

COOPER: Based on its location, Cooper Alley may have been a slave alley or highbinders' den. It still exists today, but as more of a pedestrian walkway, which dead-ends about forty-five feet into the block. A flagstone lot building or two still provide access to Jackson Street from this alley.

LEFT: This picture was taken by Cathcart in the late 1930s, a few years before the repeal of the Chinese Exclusion Act, which was the first immigration law that excluded an entire ethnic group. Although assigning quotas to all Asian immigrants was not ended until the Immigration Act of 1965, the 1930s and '40s saw the negative attitudes toward the American Chinese begin to shift. (Cathcart, 1937).

d7

BECKETT (BARTLETT) AL.: Beckett Street was originally named Bartlett Alley according to Eddy's 1849 map, after Washington Allon Bartlett, the first American alcalde of San Francisco. In 1882, it was renamed Lozier Street, which is shown on the Exclusion Act map as well as the California Historical Society copy of Cathcart's Chinatown map. In 1896, it was renamed back to Bartlett, only to be changed in the 1909 Commission on Change of Street Names to Beckett Alley. The individual for whom it was altered is still to be identified.

JACKSON ST. TH., GREAT CHINA, AH CHIC ACTOR: All of this references Chinese theater, which was practiced daily with full sets and elaborate costumes, limelights, and all the fittings. Jackson Street Theatre was also the site of several political rallies and public speaking through the 1930s and 1940s. Above "Ah Chic" is the same symbol as to the right of Emperor Norton (see box e4) and under Benny Bufano (see box d1).

RIGHT, TOP TO BOTTOM: With support from the Kuomintang, a Chinese nationalist party, the Great China Theatre opened in 1925 and was home to Chinese opera performances (Cathcart, 1937).
• *This photograph features Ah Chic, a leading Chinese tragedian, onstage in the late '30s. As Arnold Genthe explains in his book* Old Chinatown: *"Who forgets Ah Chic of the splendid, noble face, the greatest actor (I verily believe) of all his time in America— Ah Chic, who lived and died in the Jackson Street Theatre, playing seven nights a week for the pure joy of playing . . . ?" (Cathcart, 1938).*

ALL NATN.: This is probably the House of All Nations, which was a famous dance bar on the corner of Jackson and Kearny, mentioned in Asbury's *Barbary Coast*. It was run by Portuguese owner Louie Gomez from around 1910. The bar was famous for having women from all developed nations working there.

LEFT: It was estimated that San Francisco's Barbary Coast had hundreds of dance halls within a six-block radius in the first decade of the twentieth century (Cathcart, 1937).

5 POINTS: This is the name of the intersection of Columbus, Montgomery, Kearny, and Pacific. It is also the intersection of Chinatown, North Beach, the Barbary Coast, and the Financial District. The intersection itself has three triangular buildings facing it, making it a striking scene visually.

LEFT: After prohibition was repealed in 1933, recreation became increasingly important, resulting in the short-lived entertainment district International Settlement, which was popular from 1939 to 1960 (Cathcart, 1939).

BELOW: Devil's Acre, the section of Kearny Street between Pacific and Broadway in what is now North Beach, was the Barbary Coast—an area inhabited by miners, sailors, and prostitutes (Cathcart, 1939).

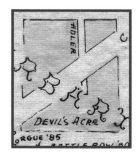

d8

DEVIL'S ACRE: This was one of the three or four original areas in the Barbary Coast that earned its horrible reputation. Liquor, prostitution, and gambling were the order of the day, unemployment was high, and corruption ran rampant. Any viable sin could be committed within this triangular street block, defined by Broadway, Kearny, and Montgomery Avenue. "The Devil's Acre" was the name used between 1873 and 1889. After that, the name seemed to drop from use, as the majority of "services" moved to Terrific Street or Pacific Avenue after 1890. When the Barbary Coast was being rebuilt after the 1906 earthquake, the Devil's Acre was replaced by middle-class businesses.

ADLER: Adler Place crosses over through Columbus (unnamed on the map). It is the site of Spec's Bar today. Though omitted on our copy of the map, the 1885 Chinatown map and the California Historical Society (CHS) map confirm that there was a temple at that location. This is unusual, as it is east of Columbus and thus considered outside the traditional boundaries of Chinatown. This and the block west of it also contain lots of inferred underground passages of old Chinatown, marked by dotted lines on the CHS copy.

d9

BROAD WAY: Broadway originated as "Broad Way," two words, because it was designed wider than most streets—sixty feet instead of forty. It led to both Cunningham's Wharf and Clarks Point, which at one time were the only docking points for all maritime businesses in early San Francisco. Broadway also housed the city jail and many of San Francisco's early hotels, and it cut into Telegraph Hill to allow access to the waterfront. Geographically, this cut stopped the Barbary Coast from moving north uphill and was later the expected end to the tall buildings of the Financial District.

PINCKNEY PL.: According to San Francisco city directories published between 1915 and 1925, it appears that Pinckney Place, a former name of this roadway, was changed to Romo Place in about 1915. The name apparently was changed to honor Fred and Eva Romo, who operated the Elinor Hotel—later the Romo Lodgings—at 31 Romo Place. It is known as Romolo Place today.

HINCKLEY: Hinckley Alley was named after William Sturgis Hinckley, alcalde of Yerba Buena from 1844 to 1846, who made sure the bridge crossed the creek at Jackson and Montgomery. This is the first documented capital improvement to the city and was greatly appreciated for shortening the distance of the walk from Portsmouth Square to Clarks Point, which was the center of all maritime activity in the mid-1800s. The alley was renamed "Fresno Alley" around 1940.

LEFT: A plaque commemorating Hinckley placed at the location of his 1844 bridge, the first for the city still known as Yerba Buena at that time. The bridge was near the intersection of Montgomery and Jackson Streets; as hard as it is to imagine it today, in the late 1840s, the original shoreline of the Bay ran right by this location (Cathcart, 1937).

OPPOSITE, TOP TO BOTTOM: A diorama from the 1939 Golden Gate International Exposition depicts the second San Francisco Committee of Vigilance, which established a new political ruling party called the People's Party. • This illustration of the Committee's roundup of James Casey and Charles Cora was published in the Illustrated London News in the June 12, 1856 issue.

Jail of '56: Here, the second San Francisco Committee of Vigilance handed over several accused individuals, community members, who were then hanged. This is the jail from which criminals James Casey and Charles Cora were given to the committee with great fanfare, supported by two hundred armed men and more than five hundred spectators and newspapers of the day. Today, it is a vacant lot. The imagery Cathcart used was from Jo Mora's diorama, *Discovery of the San Francisco Bay by Portola*, at the Golden Gate International Exposition in 1939.

e1

SMOKED FISH VENDORS AND DIM SUM DELIVERY: Although this space on the map is outside the borders of Chinatown, Cathcart makes use of it to present those stories that are the fiber of Chinatown history—in this case, the fish markets and culture surrounding cooked foods and restaurant delivery. The concept of delivered food allowed workers to keep working instead of needing lunch breaks. It was this Chinese industriousness that was so important to their attaining respect and acceptance in America, and prepared food and delivery was the most visible evidence of this trait to most outsiders. (See also box a6.)

LEFT: Food purveyors in Chinatown displayed their prepared food in the windows of their shops, which was a practice unknown outside of Chinatown at the time (Cathcart, 1937).

e2

LILIES: In Chinese culture, each flower carries its own particular symbolism based on the plant's health, delicacy, and color. *Chi*, or life energy, is conveyed symbolically through flowers, which are used in Chinese culture for special rituals and gifts. Different flowers are given for different occasions; lilies, for example, are customary gifts at weddings or for close friends. They represent unity of spirit and signify one hundred years of love. However, we have colored these flowers just as we have colored the rest of the map, so it merits mentioning that these may not be lilies at all. They may be paper-whites, which are used during the New Year's celebrations to represent the passing of the old year. They could also be irises, symbolizing what is most often translated as "the dancing spirit of early summer." This is because iris petals easily move in the wind, mimicking the fluttering of butterfly wings. Irises also have meanings of cherished friendship and promise in loving relationships. These flowers could also be narcissus, which represent the flowering of one's hidden talents and are also used in exorcisms of evil spirits.

RIGHT: Flower markets have been a fixture of Chinatown throughout its history, especially prominent at special events in the community, such as Chinese New Year. Plants symbolize growth in Chinese culture, and a flower that blooms on New Year's Day is an omen of prosperity for the coming year (Cathcart, 1938).

MOTH KITE, AS FLOWN BY A FIGURE IN PORTSMOUTH SQUARE: The popular claim is that the Chinese invented kites around 450 BCE and adopted different varieties over the millennia, starting with wood and cloth, then moving to bamboo and paper, and eventually to silk and bone or bamboo. Today, paper is used, mostly because of cost. Originally, kites were used for military purposes (such as measuring distances and sending signals) but became artistic objects in the Ming and Qing dynasties. In the United States, they were eventually used in kite-flying competitions well before Cathcart's time. Control, grace, design, and capacity to fly, dive, and attack with maneuverability were used as factors during the evaluation process. Competitions took place in Portsmouth Square, Marina Green, and the Marina Middle School field.

LEFT, TOP TO BOTTOM: A boy holds the intricately designed moth kite that directly inspired Cathcart's map illustration. Kite tails help to balance an airborne kite, initiating the graceful, fluttering dance that has been a hallmark of the Chinese kite tradition for thousands of years. • Two girls lay out kites with bird motifs. Since their invention in China over two thousand years ago, kites, which were designed to mimic a bird's natural flight, have been used for everything from fishing to signaling to sheer enjoyment. (Cathcart, 1938.)

OPPOSITE: A girl flies a bird-shaped kite during a kite-flying competition at Marina Middle School on Bay Street (Cathcart, 1938).

e3

JACK'S: This refers to a restaurant on Sacramento between Montgomery and Kearny, which was an original mainstay for San Francisco businessmen and artists alike. It opened in 1863 and remained until 2009, making it the second oldest restaurant on the West Coast after Tadich Grill (which is still serving; see box f4).

CHINESE STONE, 1852 PARROTS BLDG. AND CHINESE LABORERS: Parrott's Granite Block is a California Historical Landmark, erected by importer and banker John Parrott in 1852. The building was constructed with granite blocks imported from China, since it did not spall or splinter, and with them came qualified Chinese laborers to manage and install it. This structure survived the earthquake and fire of 1906 but was demolished in 1926. The Omni Hotel currently occupies this location.

BELOW: Parrott's Granite Block was a rarity of its time for being constructed out of granite. In 1852, the vast majority of buildings in San Francisco were entirely made of wood, which was cheap and easy to use. Parrott's, which took around ninety days to build, withstood even the 1906 earthquake and fire.

Parrott's Granite Block.

e4

THE "EMP" (EMPEROR NORTON), AT HIS HOME AT 624 COMMERCIAL STREET: Joshua Abraham Norton (born circa 1818) was a rice commodities broker who lost his mind after attempting and failing to corner the California rice market. On September 17, 1859, he declared himself Emperor of the United States, later adding "protectorate of Mexico" to his title. He was famous for making grandiose proclamations, from the dissolution of the United States to the need for a bridge between Oakland and San Francisco, and was beloved for his endearing eccentricities. Norton died on January 8, 1880; his funeral numbered over ten thousand participants and the cortege stretched over two miles. Several books and good actors have made Norton the San Francisco antihero for the twentieth and twenty-first centuries. There have been numerous campaigns to name all or part of the Bay Bridge after Norton in recognition of his original idea.

RIGHT: Emperor Norton issued currency, such as this banknote for fifty cents, for the government of which he declared himself the leader. These rare artifacts of Norton's empire are now priceless in their cultural value alone.

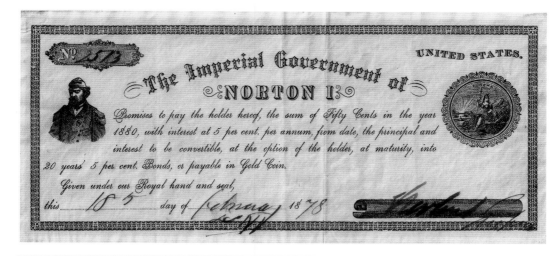

RIGHT, TOP TO BOTTOM: This 1850s illustration looks east toward the Jenny Lind Theatre, which actually became city hall during this period. • This 1850s illustration shows the devastating fire of May 1851 that wiped out the majority of the young city's buildings, including those around Portsmouth Square. The blaze, which started on the south side of Portsmouth Square, was stopped once it reached the waters of the Bay.

e5

OLD CITY HALL: The city hall was originally in the opulent and well-constructed former Jenny Lind Theatre, which the city bought from its builder, Thomas Maguire, for $200,000. The building was located at Kearny and Washington, facing west, toward Portsmouth Square, and was a hotbed of activity. All business took place within these three attached buildings, with the El Dorado on the north side and the Union to the south (both of which were gambling houses, according to *Gleason's Pictorial* from 1853). All three burned to the ground, along with five hundred other buildings in the fires of 1851, which started on the south side of Portsmouth Square.

PHILOSOPHER'S INN: This restaurant, located on Merchant Street behind the hall of justice, was in its prime during prohibition. At the time, some of its windows looked onto the old city prison and morgue.

Dunbar Al.: Dunbar Alley was lost to reconstruction on the Old City Hall site, making way for a Holiday Inn, and is now the location of the Hilton Hotel. The Chinese cultural center, the crossover bridge, and the right to public access were part of the exchange to remove a public street.

Papa Coppa No. 1, 1902; and No. 2, 1906: Coppa Restaurant opened in 1902 on the southwest corner of Montgomery and Merchant, then moved to the northeast corner of Montgomery and Merchant following the earthquake and fire of 1906. This was the great literary hangout for local writers such as Jack London, Will and Wallace Irwin, and Charles Caldwell Dobie, all of whom influenced Cathcart greatly. (Our mapmaker actually aspired to be a part of this scene.) The Irwin brothers and Dobie were the experts on pre-fire San Francisco, and the writers who frequented this place in the WPA period were Cathcart's contemporaries. Other important San Franciscans seen here were Ambrose Bierce, George Sterling, Herman Scheffauer, and James Hopper. Clarence Edwords wrote in his 1914 book, *Bohemian San Francisco*, that the Coppa had created the best chicken dish ever. (See also box f5.)

LEFT: This photograph taken not long after the 1906 earthquake shows renowned Bay Area writer Jack London and his wife Charmian riding in a car with friends outside of the original Coppa Restaurant, a favorite hangout for London and other bohemian personalities during the early twentieth century in San Francisco.

Bonini's Barn: Located at 609 Washington Street, Bonini's Barn was famous for its Bohemian Lunch. It was designed as a plank-floored restaurant using huge timber frames, as documented by a postcard from around the 1910s that shows the interior. Along with Papa Coppa and Old Grotto, these lunch counters and cafés were where Cathcart ate his daily meals, as he had no kitchen in his Montgomery Block studio.

LEFT: This early-1900s postcard depicts Bonini's Barn and its unique interior, which was designed to imitate an actual barn with horse harnesses hanging on pegs around the walls and the occasional chicken strolling across its wooden floorboards. The back of the postcard advertises the restaurant's fifty-cent "Bohemian Lunch."

e6

MEZEPPA, 1863, MAGUIRE'S THEATRE: This is a misspelling of the 1863 play *Mazeppa*, adapted from the poem of the same name by Romantic poet Lord Byron. It was performed at Maguire's Opera House, which Tom Maguire opened in 1850, but it was destroyed by the creation of Montgomery Avenue in 1871. The play *Mazeppa* premiered in San Francisco on August 27, 1863, and featured Adah Isaacs Menken, a celebrity actress of nineteenth-century theater, who rode across the stage on horseback while wearing a skin-toned costume that made her appear nude. This epitomized early San Francisco theater, with a mixture of progressiveness and scandal, as perpetuated by the Barbary Coast.

MET. TH. 1854: The Metropolitan Theatre opened at 725 Montgomery Street on Christmas Eve 1853, with J.E. Murdoch noted as the performing actor. All theater was popular in San Francisco, partly due to the lack of entertainment beyond gambling, booze, and women. Those who lived a virtuous married life only had the theater as a respectable place to take their wives. Opera, Shakespearean plays, and even Chinese theater took place in these venues. The Metropolitan was managed by Junius Brutus Booth, and his son Edwin Booth performed there as an actor. Both father and son were popular and famous in their time. Edwin's brother, John Wilkes Booth, the less successful and more disturbed of the Booth brothers, became infamous for assassinating President Abraham Lincoln. The Metropolitan Theatre was cut in half diagonally in 1871, removing the back half of the building, when Montgomery Avenue, now Columbus, was placed by eminent domain. The Metro operated until the 1906 earthquake and fire destroyed it.

RIGHT: This photo, taken by Cathcart from a second-floor window of the Montgomery Block, shows a procession with President Harry Truman coming down Columbus Avenue in 1947. The first building on the right stands on the site of the former Metropolitan Theatre, and halfway up the block on the left is Gibb Street (Cathcart, 1947).

GIBB STREET: Gibb Street is one hundred feet long and is still intact, despite considerable reconfiguration and construction since 1947. The street dead-ended at the Philippine American Cultural Center or International Hotel site. The Asian Law Caucus occupied the southern entrance, and a Hunan restaurant occupied the northern side.

129

SENTINEL BUILDING: The triangular Flatiron-style building, under construction during the 1906 earthquake and fire, was completed in 1907. It was built and owned by the corrupt politician Abe Ruef, who was prosecuted and jailed in 1907 for graft and corruption charges. It's been said the Sentinel Building wasn't completed until Ruef got out of San Quentin in 1915, but photos reveal a different story, confirming a 1907–1908 move-in date for its tenants. Falling into disrepair in the 1960s when owned by the Kingston Trio, a folk music group, the building was bought by Francis Ford Coppola in the mid-1970s. The building was renovated and restored, complete with new lighting, a cafe, and corporate offices. The ground floor is one of several important sites in North Beach where Coppola wrote the screenplays for his *Godfather* saga. His personal office occupies the top floor, in Abe Ruef's old office.

LEFT: *A view south from the Five Points intersection of Pacific, Kearny, Montgomery, and Columbus, where the triangular Sentinel Building structure stands tall. The distinctive copper-green Flatiron style was an innovative architectural statement at the turn of the twentieth century (Cathcart, 1937).*

RED MILL: Also known as the Moulin Rouge, the Red Mill was located at 555 Pacific Avenue and operated between 1906 and 1924. It was a burlesque theater, featuring stage dancers and a viewing balcony.

RIGHT: This Barbary Coast venue, located at 571 Pacific, was the site of a burlesque theater. After the 1906 earthquake and fire, the establishments in the area were rebuilt, and Pacific Avenue was once again the center of San Francisco nightlife (Cathcart, 1937).

RIGHT: While the 1906 earthquake and fire destroyed most of the Barbary Coast's red-light district, within three months, over a dozen dance halls and bars were rebuilt and operating. From 1907 until the early 1920s, Pacific Avenue, otherwise known as "Terrific Street," was home to San Francisco's bawdiest nightclubs—until prohibition put a damper on the scene. Pictured here is the Montana, as seen by Cathcart when he was exploring the area (Cathcart, 1937).

BELLA UNION: The Bella Union consisted of dance halls with girls and liquor. They were located at 557 Pacific Avenue from 1890 until the Union was destroyed by the earthquake and fire of 1906. It was rebuilt to suit an upgrade in clientele but shut down again by public opinion in 1917. The New Bella Union was a replacement of the beloved burlesque and gambling house on Portsmouth Square (box d6). This area previously housed the most dangerous Barbary Coast venues, where men were slipped mickeys by the owners or workers, and then robbed, beaten, and shanghaied into servitude. Venues rebuilt post–earthquake and fire were tourist destinations, risky only for their violation of segregation policies, morality laws, or blue laws.

MONTANA: This was another famous dive bar and dance hall at 561 Pacific Avenue, located underneath the Venetian hotel at 563, which operated into the 1950s until the International Settlement closed down. In addition to being a brothel, it housed artists and transients working in the area.

OLD HIPPODROME: It moved to 557 Pacific Avenue, the site of the former Bella Union, after having existed across the street for three decades before. We have photos from around 1937 that show the signage from the Hippodrome at 560 Pacific Avenue (see box e8). It was already in operation from around 1906 to 1925, and may have been stopped from serving liquor in 1917 like most other establishments in the area due to the war effort.

LEFT: The Hippodrome was one of the dance-hall hot spots of "Terrific Street." Pictured here is the exterior of the Hippodrome at its second location at 557 Pacific, sans its famous mythology-inspired sculptures and signage (Cathcart, 1937).

BELOW: Formerly decorating panels of the Hippodrome, Arthur Putnam's nymph-and-satyr reliefs were removed in 1937 and sold. The two winged female figures that once flanked the outside are also gone (Cathcart, 1937).

PUTNAM'S SATYRS, NYMPHS: This refers to plaster reliefs at the Old Hippodrome by sculptor Arthur Putnam (1873–1930), completed in 1907. Putnam was also known for other public sculptures, such as the concrete sphinx in Golden Gate Park outside the DeYoung Museum, and displays at both the 1915 Panama–Pacific and 1939 Golden Gate International Expositions.

PURCELLS: Originally known as the "So Different Club," Purcell's Café was established at 520 Pacific Avenue by two African American former Pullman porters, Lew Purcell and Sam King, and operated between 1907 and 1919. Although a black-owned business, it was integrated racially and thus called a "black-and-tan" club for this diversity. A jazz dance club with taxi dancing (paid dance partners), it was a raucous experience instrumental in the creation of San Francisco jazz music, culture, and dancing. King hired pianist Sid LeProtti early on and made him musical director for the house band, which hired African Americans from all over the United States, creating a hotbed of creativity in jazz music and dance.

Purcell's Globe Theater was highlighted as "The Best Colored Show in Town" and was a well-known African American club of the post-1906 Barbary Coast. It was another black-and-tan club within segregated San Francisco, located at 551 Pacific Avenue, and was described as a place to "come down and slum it." It taught white visitors the Grizzly Bear and other ragtime-based dances of the time. Since they didn't serve liquor, the dance halls could remain open after 1914, and many of these did so until the late 1920s, when the laws changed again.

RIGHT: Purcell's Globe Theater, a multiracial jazz club, advertises itself in language characteristic of the times (Cathcart, 1937).

"BOTTLE" MEYERS: Potentially refers to an establishment called Bottle Koenig's, an old beer hall of the Barbary Coast. It had a famous owner and was written about in Asbury's *Barbary Coast*.

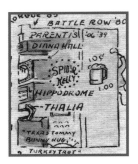

MORGUE '85: In March of 1885, the Board of Supervisors funded and passed legislation to provide for the construction and maintenance of a city and county morgue. This has nothing to do with that. A story in Gary Paul Lukas's book *Seven Years in Sodom* tells of a bartender at an underground dive saloon called the Slaughterhouse ending happy hour by smashing a bottle on the head of a drunk patron, likely killing him, and announcing that the place would be called "The Morgue" from then on. There are a few stories of people being killed in this manner. Other weapons used were blackjacks, lead pipes, or bags of rocks. This venue was a hangout of criminals known for using such "tools" and was one of the places even the police wouldn't go.

LEFT: *The Morgue was located beneath the site of Parente's, a dive saloon run by boxing enthusiast Louie Parente. In 1922, Parente also built an equally sketchy hotel in El Verano, which contained a secret brothel and underground casino (Cathcart, 1937).*

BATTLE ROW '80S: This was located on the east side of Kearny Street from Pacific to Broadway, across from the Devil's Acre. For thirty years, troublemakers assembled to drink, whore, and commit crimes from around 1860 until the late 1880s. All of this necessitated an attempt to soften this region, plagued by theft, kidnapping, extortion, opium trade, and prostitution. The Devil's Acre, Battle Row, and Murderer's Corner were all within the original Barbary Coast and were areas that helped establish this illicit reputation for more than fifty years. Despite the creation of less dangerous venues in the Terrific Street period of the 1890s, like the 560 Pacific Hippodrome, the number of saloons was greater than five thousand packed within these few blocks. Spaces as small as closets and underground cribs were rented out for top dollar, with a piece of most deals going to pay off law enforcement authorities.

PARENTI'S '06–'39: Parente's (note the spelling) was located at 592 Pacific Avenue at the Five Points corner, right above the site of the former "Morgue." A café serving pisco punch in the Barbary Coast tradition, it opened in 1906 and operated until the International Settlement (the rebranding of the Barbary Coast) in 1939. The place was covered with boxing photos and memorabilia from the nineteenth and early twentieth centuries.

DIANA HALL: This was a theater located at 580 Pacific Avenue. The building still stands and is preserved as a landmark, as are many other rebuilt 1906 buildings.

OPPOSITE: *Diana Hall, also known as Diana Café, moved its location along Pacific Avenue at least three times. Here, one of its locations at 580 Pacific—formerly the original site of the Thalia—is shown for lease (Cathcart, 1937).*

Spider Kelly: Spider Kelly was established in 1909 at 574 Pacific Avenue by James Curtin, a pugilistic Irishman. He took possession of a space formerly known as the Seattle Saloon, established in 1852, which was notorious for its bartenders and girls robbing its patrons. It was especially famous for the "door key" scam of giving patrons prepaid keys to locks that didn't exist. Later in the nineteenth century, this space became a drag bar offering the same services as the other venues, but with men in drag for gay men. Spider Kelly developed a business so beloved for its contribution to having a good time that numerous articles and, of course, Asbury's book, *The Barbary Coast*, discusses the joys of spending time here.

LEFT: The building formerly housing Spider Kelly's awaits new tenants shortly before the development of the International Settlement entertainment district in the late '30s (Cathcart, 1937).

Hippodrome: This is the original site at 560 Pacific Avenue, opened during the original Terrific Street period in 1890, as a first attempt to clean up Battle Row and make sure more people felt comfortable coming to this area (although it was still dangerous). It was used as a setting for a 1919 silent film. In 1934, after prohibition ended, the 560 Hippodrome reopened for a short period and eventually became the Monaco Restaurant in 1939, moving the old sign across the street to 557. It is apparent that there were two Hippodromes operating from around 1920 to 1937.

LEFT; Looking west down the 500 block, past Columbus into the 600 block of Pacific Avenue, shows us the same assortment of buildings that still exists today (Cathcart, 1937).

RIGHT: *The emblem of a chariot racer, shown on the arched entrance to the Old Hippodrome, is a reference to the name of the establishment, which originally referred to ancient Greek or Roman courses for horse or chariot races (Cathcart, 1937).*

Thalia: When the Thalia Theater opened at 580 Pacific Avenue in 1911, it was the largest dance hall on Pacific Avenue, with six bartenders and one hundred waitresses (or prostitutes). It is also considered the birthplace of the Turkey Trot and Texas Tommy dances, which created nationwide dance crazes in the early part of the century. It moved to 514½ Pacific Avenue in 1913. The establishment became a "dance academy" to teach patrons how to "dance" in order to bypass the Red Light Abatement Act, which forbade taxi dances after 1921. This move allowed the venue to remain open and served as a model for other establishments in Chicago, Baltimore, and elsewhere to avoid being shut down by law enforcement authorities.

RIGHT: *Shown at 514½ Pacific in 1911 or 1912, the Thalia was named for either the muse of comedy or the goddess of banquets in Greek mythology, likely a reference to its rowdy atmosphere.*

TEXAS TOMMY, BUNNY HUG, TURKEY TROT: These are the famous dances invented in San Francisco's Barbary Coast. The African American community helped create these popular dances, which then spread across the nation. *Tommy* and *bunny* are period slang for prostitutes, and newspapers attempted to sway public opinion toward banning the first two listed dances on a national level based on their name, as the reform movements of this era believed that dancing could lead to sin. However, after San Franciscans viewed these dances, they did not consider them offensive.

10¢ OR $1.00 BEER PINT ICON: This might be a reference to a sign once hanging on the street, possibly showing the price of a prostitute and a beer.

LEFT: Even after Spider Kelly's closed, the signage remained undisturbed for years before Cathcart photographed it. This one advertises dancers showcasing a popular but formerly controversial dance, the Texas Tommy (Cathcart, 1937).

<table>
<tr><td>e9</td></tr>
</table>

***Barbary Coast* by Herbert Asbury:** Published in 1933, this is the most influential book for Cathcart's Barbary Coast area of the map. We believe the information provided a starting point for his research into the businesses and buildings of this era. Our photos show a transitional space between periods of prohibition, economic depression, and closed locations from 1937 to 1938. Just twenty-five years before this map was created, the Barbary Coast was the center of all entertainment activity in San Francisco, and had been for more than seventy-five years. This classic book was written four years before Cathcart moved to San Francisco and may have influenced his decision to move here from Seattle.

From around 1894 to 1897, there were more than 3,000 licensed bars and 1,175 dance halls within this three-block area, and all of the activity was driven by prostitution, oftentimes masked as dancing and accessible through back doors, underground passageways, and second-story cribs via back stairs. When the police shut down the Barbary Coast after the Red Light Abatement Act went into effect in 1917, authorities refused access to any person in the area without legitimate purpose. The Barbary Coast bars and brothels paid a large sum of protection money to the police and corrupt city officials over the years of its operation. Many prostitutes evicted from the Barbary Coast went to Oakland, while others moved to less populated locations, including new establishments in the Sierra Nevada Gold Country.

RIGHT: This establishment advertising rooms at 438 Pacific may once have been a hotel, but it fell into disrepair by 1937 (Cathcart, 1937).

MAN IN OLD GARB: A historically accurate traditional outfit in homage to Arnold Genthe photos and the pre-1906 Chinatown resident, still evident but not so common by 1947.

LEFT: This 1903 photo shows the formally dressed leaders of the Chinese Consolidated Benevolent Association—better known as the Six Companies—which played a significant role (sometimes positive, sometimes negative) in facilitating immigration to Chinatown by coordinating with American employers who wished to use Chinese labor despite the restrictions of the Chinese Exclusion Act.

"GOLD MOUNTAIN BIG CITY" SIGN IN CHINESE CHARACTERS: San Francisco has the distinction of being "Big City" (*Dai Fow*), while Sacramento is "Second City" (*Yee Fow*) and Stockton is "Third City" (*Sam Fow*). These monikers, applied by the Chinese community, are based on the size of their respective Chinatowns. Cathcart has given the top character, "gold," extra strokes on its roof, which may have been put there to make it look more "Oriental" to a 1940s Western audience. However, it merits repeating that this map was reviewed and vetted by Cathcart's hosts and friends in Chinatown before it was published, which indicates some degree of acceptance on the part of the Chinese business community to help promote Chinatown.

LEFT: An 1850 drawing looks out toward the Bay over Portsmouth Square, the main central square in San Francisco during the Gold Rush years. Chinatown would develop around Portsmouth Square, which remains a lively park to this day, bordered by Washington, Kearny, and Clay Streets.

BELOW: This unique early streetcar from the 1870s was designed by Henry Casebolt and dubbed the "balloon car." Its circular body rotated when the car reached the end of a line, making for an easy change of direction.

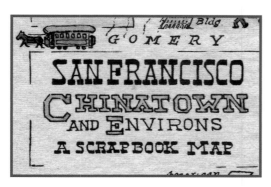

f2 / f3

SAN FRANCISCO
CHINATOWN AND
ENVIRONS: A
SCRAPBOOK MAP:
Cathcart's self-defining style, as a scrapbook map.

SINGLE HORSE-DRAWN STREET CAR ON MONTGOMERY STREET: The first system of trams and trolleys had horses pulling trolley cars along a track system built at the cost of the company. The level ground of Montgomery Street had one of the first lines, which was operational as early as 1858. It was these first horse-drawn trolleys that inspired the mechanized cable cars. This was largely due to the fact that horses were not able to climb the steep hills of San Francisco and often slipped when attempting to haul heavy loads of dirt or cobblestone, potentially injuring the horses and damaging the load.

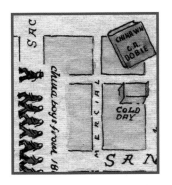

f4

CHINA BOYS FROM 1863–80: A term originally applied to the Chinese after a thank-you from the Chinese community was signed "China boys." This was in response to a ceremony welcoming them to San Francisco in August 1850 by Mayor John Geary. Sacramento Street, also known as "China Street" or "Tong Yen Guy," was the original Chinatown. A filthy place unwanted by white San Franciscans, it was among the first sites where Chinese lived from 1848 on, and through segregation and the Exclusion Act became the center of all legitimate Chinese business as well as crime and prostitution for the first forty years. Sacramento Street was also the street with the most white prostitutes into the 1890s, as shown on San Francisco's 1885 map.

LEFT: Two traditionally dressed residents cross the street from a ubiquitous corner market. Street markets have played a central role in the business and culture of Chinatown from the earliest days of its development along Sacramento Street, their crowded fronts drawing in visitors seeking both the licit and the illicit (Cathcart, 1938).

CHINATOWN BY CHARLES CALDWELL DOBIE: Published in 1936, while the Exclusion Act was still in effect, this was perhaps the second most influential book for Cathcart. This is a book about San Francisco's Chinatown based on the personal narrative of Dobie observing the Chinese during his childhood in the early 1900s, then transitioning to his later adulthood in which he could articulate both the historical and contemporary outlook on the Chinese in California. His book is more or less written from the perspective that the Chinese were essential to the workforce and adapted to living in San Francisco despite recognizing that they'd never become citizens. Dobie was influenced by the work of Arnold Genthe and references him frequently. Many of the terms and the language used in Dobie's book are reiterated by Cathcart in his map, such as "an old podii" (see box c4). The book is illustrated by E.H. Suydam, a well-known artist who worked on many of Dobie's publications. Many scenes in Cathcart's photography emulate Suydam's illustrations.

COLD DAY: Cold Day was a restaurant on 545 Clay that was established by three Croatian immigrants in 1849, originally as a coffee stand. It was first called the New World Coffee Saloon before its name changed to the Cold Day Restaurant, which came from a quote by 1880s tax assessor Alexander Badlam, who boasted that it would be "a cold day" when he was defeated and then lost his reelection. By Cathcart's time, the restaurant had officially been renamed the Tadich Grill. At 240 California Street since 1967, the Tadich Grill is still in operation and is the oldest restaurant in town.

OPPOSITE: The cover of Charles Caldwell Dobie's book on Chinatown featuring the art of illustrator E.H. Suydam. Both Dobie's writing and Suydam's drawings greatly influenced Cathcart's approach in the creation of his map.

SAN FRANCISCO'S
CHINATOWN

EH Suydam
Old Chinatown 19

BY CHARLES CALDWELL DOBIE
ILLUSTRATED BY E. H. SUYDAM

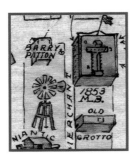

f5

BARRY & PATTON: This was a popular resort at 606 Montgomery Street, which—according to a 1902 article in the *San Francisco Call* newspaper—was the saloon that writer Bret Harte frequented, where he was usually seen drinking alone. Considered cold or antisocial, Harte was remembered for being a quiet wallflower, keeping to himself and watching others play billiards or poker, or maintaining his manuscripts and notes.

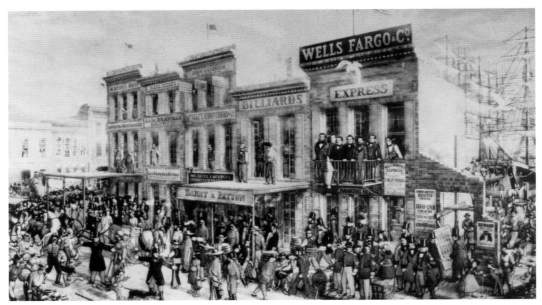

LEFT: This illustration from the early 1850s shows raucous crowds along Montgomery Street, commensurate with the diversity of establishments comprising its storefronts. The Barry & Patton saloon, which writer Brett Harte frequented, is flanked by the very first Wells Fargo office (in the same spot occupied by their main headquarters today) as well as the offices of the San Francisco Herald two buildings down.

NIANTIC: The *Niantic* arrived at 11 P.M. on July 5, 1849, and docked at what is now 505 Sansome Street. The *Niantic* was the earliest vessel to arrive with gold prospectors, headed to the Sierra Nevada gold fields. It was also the most inland buried ship in San Francisco's downtown area and was used as a hotel, then a storeship, for the goods of commission agents. Similar vessels, such as the *Apollo* and *General Harrison*, also became storeships until they were destroyed in the fire of May 3–4, 1851. This part of town was built upon the sunken hulls of stripped vessels, which were tied up to the existing piers, cored, sunk, and then filled with all sorts of garbage, debris, and sand until level with the waterline. Once this process was sufficiently followed, the pier was then removed and built further out, and the same practice proceeded to fill in that newly cleared area, thus creating the first landfill.

LEFT: The improvised conversion of the Niantic and the Apollo into places of business along Sansome Street is shown in this Gold Rush–era illustration. The Niantic was estimated to have earned her owners upwards of $20,000 per month during her time as a storeship.

BELOW: *The iconic Montgomery Block had a colorful history that played host to everything from prosperous businesses to Bohemian artists to invaluable archives (which were protected by its fireproof walls). This photo by Cathcart was used in the 1940s to promote efforts to save the building—efforts that eventually proved unsuccessful, as it was finally torn down in 1959, over a century after its construction (Cathcart, 1946).*

WINDMILL: Used frequently on Telegraph Hill and along the shorelines to pump water for assorted purposes, one of which was to water the potato patch in Portsmouth Square in early 1835.

1853 M.B.: The Montgomery Block, at 628 Montgomery Street, was the first fireproof building in San Francisco, built in 1853 and first named the Washington Block, as per the 1854 Bridgens/Bixby map. It had iron shutters and brick walls forty inches thick. It was the predecessor of more than thirty "block" buildings in San Francisco and originally consisted of high-end offices for lawyers working in land law and surveyors resolving the land disputes in California around the ranchos. It later became the epicenter of San Francisco's twentieth-century art scene through WPA grants for tenants, live-work setups, and civil rights lawyers. Dong Kingman, Charles Preuss, Robert Stackpole, and Cathcart were tenants here. Sun Yat-sen is believed to have written the Constitution for the Chinese Republic, established in 1912, here. The building survived many fires as promised, including the fire after the 1906 earthquake. Eventually, it was lost to real estate speculation and torn down in 1959, precipitating the creation of "the end" of the Financial District at the south side of Washington Street. Presently, it is the site of a newer landmark: the Transamerica Pyramid.

BANK EXCHANGE: The Bank Exchange Saloon was the first tenant of the Montgomery Block, opened by Duncan Nicol in 1853, and remained in business until prohibition was enacted in 1919. Nicol invented San Francisco's famed pisco punch here and served it from a proprietary recipe, supposedly lost upon his death.

PISCO PUNCH, 2 FOR 25¢: This was the cocktail most closely associated with San Francisco since its invention in 1853. It was made from Peruvian brandy, bitters, and exotic ingredients such as pineapple juice. This was considered the drink of San Francisco, from the Barbary Coast to Nob Hill, into the 1940s. Tourists sought out places serving pisco with the same devotion shown toward other San Franciscan experiences such as cable cars, sourdough bread, and crab. In Cathcart's time, Parente's was famous for having great pisco punch and operated until around 1939 (see box e8).

LEFT, TOP TO BOTTOM: The Barbary Coast was San Francisco's world-famous vice district, and pisco punch was its most iconic drink. Offering the drink became a key selling point for renowned establishments such as Parente's. It is believed that part of the drink's legendary potency was due to the inclusion of a "mystery ingredient" that included coca leaves, the main component in cocaine. • A plaque mounted on the side of the Montgomery Block commemorated the invention of pisco punch by bartender Duncan Nicol at the building's Bank Exchange saloon. Nicol's original recipe was presumed lost for many years after he died in 1926, but thankfully, an extant copy of the recipe was found in the early 1970s and subsequently published to preserve the famous drink's legacy. (Cathcart, 1937)

OLD GROTTO: The Old Grotto restaurant, located at 545 Washington Street, was a favorite haunt for Cathcart and many of the WPA artists in his time. Historian Kevin Starr mentioned the Old Grotto as a place to get a full dinner for fifty to seventy-five cents, as his parents enjoyed it in the late 1930s.

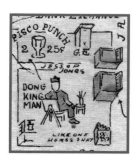

f6

G.E.: The *Golden Era* building at 732 Montgomery was built in 1851 and housed one of the early printed newspapers of California, called the *Golden Era*, from 1852 to 1856, of which Bret Harte was an editor. Mark Twain and other notable authors of the time were contributors. Also featured on the 1854 San Francisco map in Cathcart's possession, this was of monumental importance to our mapmaker, as he was a fan of these two men and their relationship to the city. In Cathcart's time, the Washington Broom Company was located here. This textile manufacturer of overalls was representative of the industries into which Chinese people were allowed to enter. The second-floor studio was rented to Maynard Dixon, a well-known twentieth-century painter, and farther down the block was the Black Cat, which eventually became a hub of gay culture.

RIGHT: 732 Montgomery Street had housed many different businesses by the time Cathcart took this shot, not long after he moved into the Montgomery Block just down the street. The building was designated as an official city landmark in 1969 and still looks much the same today (Cathcart, 1939).

JESSOP JONES: Jessop Jones Alley, now called Hotaling Place, was renamed for Anson Parsons Hotaling. He originally built a building on the corner of Jackson and Jessop Jones in 1866 as a hotel, but soon went into the whiskey business. His success led him to build a second whiskey warehouse across from Jessop Jones on Jackson. His first was at 451 Jackson Street with the annex at 455. They still stand because Parsons's sons, who were on-site during the firestorm of April 18, 1906, were allegedly able to convince General Funston (who was in charge of dynamiting buildings to prevent the spread of fire) not to dynamite their warehouses because it would simply spread the fire. Funston was convinced and instead moved the whiskey, saving the entire block with a mile-long hose extending from the bay. The Hotaling building, made with brick and cast-iron facades, was an Italianate design, popluar in commercial structures in the late-nineteenth century. It's said that this was one of the buildings looted by federal troops after saving the Appraisers Building down the block. (See also quote in box f7).

LEFT: Despite its proximity to the old Barbary Coast district, Jackson Street in the late 1930s had become utilitarian in function, a mere shadow of the hive of activity it once was. Despite the repeal of prohibition in 1933, the crackdown on San Francisco's vice districts changed the neighborhood for good (Cathcart, 1937).

RIGHT: This panel from a 1949 magazine titled Pay Dirt! San Francisco: The Romance of a Great City, which celebrated the centennial of the Gold Rush, shows famous Chinese American watercolor artist Dong Kingman, whose urban paintings often featured San Francisco's Chinatown in the mid-twentieth century.

BELOW: The explosion at Jackson and Sansome created a vacant spot on Cathcart's map, and in fact, it remains a parking lot to this day. The first building to occupy the spot in the 1850s was a warehouse owned by prominent San Francisco businessmen Henry and John Cowell (Cathcart, 1937).

DONG KINGMAN: Dong Kingman (1911–2000) was a Chinese American artist. He used watercolors to create urban scenes and worked in the Montgomery Block and on the streets on this map. He was born in Oakland and was greatly involved in many Chinese American communities around the country, and associated with both the San Francisco and New York art scene.

BUILDING ON CORNER OF SANSOME AND WASHINGTON STREETS: The icon appears to be a mortar and pestle, possibly indicating an apothecary.

EMPTY LOT WITH RUBBLE ON THE CORNER OF JACKSON AND SANSOME: An explosion at this site in 1937 or 1938 sent two water tanks hurtling through the air several blocks away, where they hit the Montgomery Block and leveled the corner building. This lot is still vacant since it had not been rebuilt at the time, with the expectation that the Financial District would continue being built up to Broadway, two blocks away. It's now historic.

"LIKE ONE-HORSE SHAY": This is a quote referencing Oliver Wendell Holmes's 1858 poem "The Deacon's Masterpiece, or the Wonderful One-Hoss Shay," about a one-horse chaise—a two-wheeled, single-horsed surrey for women—which was built by a pious preacher with great pride. It survived to its hundredth year, then spontaneously fell apart at every joint and structure and collapsed into an irreparable pile of rubble. This is a witty reference to the total collapse of the building shown.

ARTIST DONG KINGMAN discusses a creative point with students sketching Chinatown. Born in California, and educated in China, Mr. Kingman is famous for his water colors.

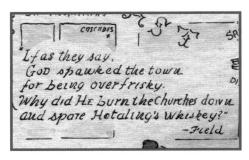

f7 / f8

CASCADES: The Cascade, located at the corner of Montgomery and Pacific, was a saloon or hall referenced in Asbury's *Barbary Coast*. It is marked with an *X* like the restaurant Jack's, possibly indicating another favorite lunch spot for artist and authors.

"IF AS THEY SAY, GOD SPANKED THE TOWN FOR BEING OVERFRISKY, WHY DID HE BURN THE CHURCHES DOWN AND SPARE HOTALING'S WHISKEY?"—FIELD: This is a San Francisco poem created by Charles Field as a dismissive response to the national puritan attitude that the great earthquake and fire of 1906 was God's punishment for San Francisco's sinful ways, particularly represented by Hotaling's whiskey storage warehouses located in the Barbary Coast. (See also box f6.)

LEFT: This view east on Pacific Avenue shows the Cascade, the second building on the right. Pacific Avenue was once home to many infamous Barbary Coast venues, including saloons and brothels, but by the time this photograph was taken, Pacific Avenue was home to much tamer establishments, such as factory warehouses (Cathcart, 1937).

f9

SANGUINETTIE'S FOR 50 CENTS, DINNER WITH WINE, 1900S: Stefano Sanguinetti (1847–1918) opened his diner in 1888 at 5 Vallejo Street, between Davis and Front. Initially, his customers were dock workers from the Union Street wharf eating "four-bit plates" (fifty cents) of spaghetti with a chunk of French bread and a pint of dago red, all for fifty cents. Later, in the 1890s, author/poet George Sterling, muralist and historian Maynard Dixon or his wife, beloved San Francisco artist Dorothea Lange, and their pals discovered Sanguinetti's as a place to celebrate financial success. It's said they usually ate at "two-bit houses," where a platter and pint could be had for just twenty-five cents. It burned down on April 19, 1906, with the rest of the neighborhood.

Sanguinetti John, waiter, r. 58 Tehama
Sanguinetti Julio, blacksmith, r. 607 Greenwich
Sanguinetti Leon, secretary S. F. Hay and Grain Co.,
    619–621 Fourth, r. 1425 Kearny
Sanguinetti Luigi, clerk, r. 1425 Kearny
Sanguinetti Luigi, laborer Am. Salt Co.
Sanguinetti S. (Sanguinetti & Co.) r. 257 Davis
Sanguinetti Stefano, r. 1600 Stockton
Sanguinetti & Co (S. Sanguinetti, Bernard Perata and
    A. Del Monte) restaurant and liquors, SW cor Pacific and Davis
Sanitarium Baths, Cornelius E. Driscoll proprietor, 2212
    Powell

LEFT: A section of Langley's 1889 city directory shows us the residences of contemporary San Franciscans with the surname "Sanguinetti." S. Sanguinetti, the proprietor of Sanguinetti's diner marked on the map, lived at 1600 Stockton.

g1

FAN TAN: Fan-Tan is a card game invented in the third century in China that spread in use over 1,500 years. In San Francisco, it was the most popular Chinese card game in the nineteenth and early twentieth centuries. In 1889, there were over fifty Fan-Tan houses with anywhere from two to twenty-five tables, depending on the size of the room. These shops were always busy and had considerable pressure from competitors opening new houses.

g2

WASH HOUSE AND CHINESE INDUSTRIES OF 1860S–1890S WITH SHOES, OVERALLS, AND CIGARS: These icons represent some businesses and jobs from which Chinese were not excluded based on the Exclusion Act. These service industries included occupations such as cobbler, shoe repairman, tailor, cigar roller, and launderer. Thus, they were viewed as their only path to prosperity, health, and good humor, and as a means to support family through work and a balanced life.

RIGHT: This laundry, located on Waverly Place, is one of many family-owned businesses founded in pursuit of an honorable life, in accordance with both traditional values and the few trades permitted for Chinese immigrants prior to the repeal of the Exclusion Act (Cathcart, 1938).

g3

AMERICAN THEATRE 1852 A CHINESE PLAY GIVEN: The American Theatre was a two-thousand-seat theater built at the waterline on Sansome Street by Dr. D. G. "Yankee" Robinson in 1851. The theater was an immediate success and remained open for many years, despite being upstaged by its biggest competitor, Maguire's Opera House. Nonetheless, the American Theatre held a performance of a Chinese play in 1852, prior to the exclusions of the 1870s, and was renowned for the quality of the performance and striking drama. It sold out for its full run of four shows. (See also box e6.)

BELOW: A hand-drawn illustration by Cathcart shows the American Theatre. Built on a foundation of mud and landfill, it is said to have sunk three inches on opening night, sustaining the weight of the audience (Cathcart, 1946).

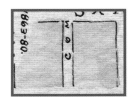

g4

COMMERCIAL ST.: Bordering the infamous Barbary Coast and leading to Chinatown, Commercial Street was the Financial District at the time, as it remains today.

1ST BK. PTD. IN CAL. 1849, *LIFE IN CALIFORNIA*: Cathcart mistakenly refers to *Life in California* as being the first book printed in California. It was actually published and printed in New York City in 1846 and, along with the 1840 book *Two Years Before the Mast* by Richard Henry Dana, may be among the earliest California experiences conveyed firsthand. The first book printed in California was in fact *Manifesto a la República Mejicana*, published by Augustin Zambrano in 1835. The first book published specifically in English in California was an 1849 book called *California As It Is, and As It May Be* by Felix Wierzbicki. It was published by Washington Montgomery Bartlett, first American Alcade of San Francisco, and printed at 8 Clay Street, exactly where our icon has been placed.

A MAN WITH A QUEUE, CARRYING A CRATE: Called a "basketman" in the photographic record, this is a reference to the public perception of the general nature of the Chinese in California—carrying something to promote, with lots of attention paid to imported goods from China to service local commercial needs. This included granite and brick needed for buildings constructed in San Francisco after the groundbreaking construction of the Parrott's Granite Block in 1852 (see box e3). Imported materials were taxed in the Appraisers Building.

RIGHT: Former Polish revolutionary turned San Franciscan gold miner Felix Wierzbicki wrote California As It Is and As It May Be *as a guide to California. Shown here are pages from the Grabhorn Press 1933 reissue of the book.*

BELOW: A basketman carries goods along a bustling Chinatown street. Chinatown's inhabitants were well known for efficient transportation of products on foot (Cathcart, 1938).

g6

Appraisers Bldg.: The Appraisers Building at 630 Sansome, originally constructed with brick and granite in 1874, was fireproofed and saved in the 1906 earthquake and fire by the United States military. It has been used for the appraisals of imported goods, customs, and immigration since its opening. Today, this is the place where citizenship paperwork is filed. The structure represented on this map was torn down in 1938 and replaced in 1939 on the same site with the present building performing the same functions as the old one, just on a larger scale.

LEFT: The Appraisers Building, formerly known as the Custom House, is one of only a few buildings that remained intact after the 1906 earthquake and fire. The United States Army saved the building from the flames after a struggle of several hours.

g7

Empty banner with a Chinese character meaning "map" above: On the version of the map in the California Historical Society's collection, this banner has Ken Cathcart's name written in it. It was left blank on our version because it was an uncompleted artist's proof.

LEFT: On the California Historical Society's completed version of this map, the character and banner in this space proudly display Cathcart's name (Cathcart, 1947).

g8

A mariner, carrying crates off a boat: San Francisco is a maritime city, with seamen and the goods and services that went along with it, good and bad. Most people arriving in the city prior to 1870 arrived by sea, and all business was done via trade routes established during the 1835 to 1855 maritime era. Most San Franciscans had working knowledge of and were literate in maritime nomenclature well into the twentieth century.

g9

Chess: This game of strategy and imperial domination was invented in India around the seventh century, but some attribute its creation to the Chinese instead. Regardless of its exact origins, the game has been practiced and enjoyed by the Chinese for millennia. The current pieces are based on Spanish models from the fifteenth century, with present rules established in the nineteenth century. Chess is still played daily at Portsmouth Square, and the Mechanics' Institute spends over $100,000 a year on teaching chess to people of all ages, men and women, girls and boys.

OPPOSITE, TOP TO BOTTOM: A group of seamen gathers to discuss the day's work, likely in one of the ports of San Francisco Bay. The sailor portrayed on the map is shown coming from the direction of the bay, which was a hub of maritime activity from the earliest days of the city (Cathcart, 1938).
• Children pass the time with checkers, traditionally seen as a "gateway" game to chess, which has a rich history in both San Francisco and China (Cathcart, 1937).

REFERENCES

Asbury, Herbert. *The Barbary Coast: An Informal History of the San Francisco Underworld*. New York: Alfred A. Knopf, 1933.

Atherton, Gertrude. *The Splendid Idle Forties: Stories of Old California*. New York: Macmillan Company, 1902.

Bailey, Paul. *Sam Brannan and the California Mormons*. Los Angeles: Westernlore Press, 1943.

Bell, Hudson. "Ross Alley & the Truth about Chinatown's side streets." *Fern Hill Times*, June 28, 2016. https://fernhilltoursdot-com.wordpress.com/2016/06/28/ross-alley-the-truth-about-chinatowns-side-streets/.

British Pathé. "War Relief from Chinatown's Lner (1938)." YouTube, April 13, 2014. https://www.youtube.com/watch?v=cozB2TTRYSw.

Brown, D. Mackenzie, ed. *China Trade days in California: Selected Letters from the Thompson Collection*. Berkeley: UC Press, 1947.

Burke, Thomas. *Limehouse Nights: Tales of Chinatown*. London: Grant Richards Limited, 1916.

Campbell, Maury B., ed. *Pay Dirt! San Francisco: The Romance of a Great City*. Vigilante Publications, 1949.

Chan, Anthony. *Perpetually Cool: The Many Lives of Anna May Wong*. Scarecrow Press, 2007.

Chinese Symbolism and Its Associated Beliefs. Quon-Quon, Co. 1945.

Chinn, Thomas W., ed. *A History of The Chinese in California; A Syllabus*. San Francisco: Chinese Historical Society of America, 1969.

Cleugh, James. *A History of Oriental Orgies*. New York: Crown Publishers Inc., 1968.

Dana, Richard Henry, Jr. *Two Years Before the Mast*. Harper and Brothers, 1840.

Davis, William Heath. *Sixty years in California, a history of events and life in California; personal, political and military, under the Mexican regime; during the quasi-military government of the territory by the United States, and after the admission of the state into the union, being a compilation by a witness of the events described*. San Francisco: A. J. Leary, 1889.

Dillon, Richard, *The Hatchet Men: The Story of the Tong Wars in San Francisco's Chinatown*. New York: Coward-McCann, Inc., 1962.

Dobie, Charles Caldwell. *San Francisco: A Pageant*. D. Appleton-Century Company, Incorporated, 1939.

———. *San Francisco's Chinatown*. D. Appleton-Century Company, 1936.

Dowd, Katie. "Sex and 'slummers' balconies': The brief, wild days of San Francisco's 'Terrific Street.'" *SFGate*, March 22, 2018. https://www.sfgate.com/bayarea/article/history-of-terrif-ic-street-san-francisco-clubs-12774948.php.

Edwords, Clarence E. *Bohemian San Francisco*. Paul Elder, 1914.

Elliott, Jeff. "The Village of Vice in the Valley of the Moon." *Santa Rosa History*. July 3, 2016. http://santarosahistory.com/word-press/2016/07/the-village-of-vice-in-the-valley-of-the-moon/.

Erenberg, Lewis A. *Steppin' Out: New York Nightlife and the Transformation of American Culture, 1890–1930*. Chicago University of Chicago Press, 1984.

Federal Writers Project of the Works Progress Administration. *San Francisco in the 1930s: The WPA Guide to the City by the Bay*. Berkeley: University of California Press, Apr 5, 2011.

Figueroa, José. *Manifesto a la República Mejicana*. Monterey, 1835.

Gaskell, C. A. *The C. A. Gaskell Family and Business Atlas of the World*. Chicago: John F. Waite, 1895.

Genthe, Arnold and Will Irwin. *Old Chinatown: A Book of Pictures*. New York: Mitchell Kennerley, 1908.

Gentry, Curt. *The Madams of San Francisco*. New York: Doubleday & Co, 1964.

Gillespie, Charles. "Letter to Thomas Larkin." San Francisco City Archives, March 6, 1848.

Hartman, Sierra. "A Rare Look at the Tunnels Under San Francisco." *The Bold Italic*, Nov 25, 2013. https://thebolditalic.com/a-rare-look-at-the-tunnels-under-san-francisco-the-bold-italic-san-francisco-896f850dd994?gi=2398c83fddd0.

Hom, Gloria Sun, ed. *Chinese Argonauts: An Anthology of the Chinese Contributions to the Historical Development of Santa Clara County*. Los Altos Hills, California: Foothill Community College, 1971.

Irwin, Wallace. *Chinatown Ballads*. New York: Duffield & Company, 1906.

Jackson, Joseph Henry. *Anybody's Gold: The Story of California's Mining Towns*. New York: D. Appleton-Century Company, 1941.

Kamiya, Gary. "Saga and assassination of Chinatown's 'Little Pete.'" *San Francisco Chronicle*. July 12, 2013. https://www.sfchronicle.com/bayarea/article/Saga-and-assassination-of-China-town-s-Little-4663076.php.

———. "Iconic SF building was home to Bohemians for decades. Then it was destroyed." *San Francisco Chronicle*. October 26, 2018. https://www.sfchronicle.com/chronicle_vault/article/Icon-ic-SF-building-was-home-to-Bohemians-for-13340080.php.

Khan, Bethany. "Pigtail of a Disgraced Chinese Man." *Museums Worcestershire*, July 20, 2016. https://researchworcestershire.wordpress.com/2016/07/20/pigtail-of-a-disgraced-chinese-man./

Koeppel, Geri. "Plugged In: The Fascinating History of the Chinese Telephone Exchange." *Hoodline*, April 18, 2016. https://hood-line.com/2016/04/plugged-in-the-fascinating-history-of-the-chinese-telephone-exchange.

Lee, Anthony W. *Picturing Chinatown: Art and Orientalism in San Francisco*. Berkeley: UC Press, 2001.

Lewis, Oscar. *The Big Four*. Comstock Book Distributors, 1985.

Low, Henry. *Cook at Home in Chinese*. New York: The Macmillan Company, 1938.

Lukas, Gary Paul. *Seven Years in Sodom*. Xulon Press, 2010.

The Maritime Heritage Project. "Little Pete (Fung Jing Toy, Fong Ching)." https://www.maritimeheritage.org/news/Chinese-Little-Pete.html.

McDannold, Thomas A. "The Bay Area." *California's Chinese Heritage: A Legacy of Places* (blog). June 2017. https://www.californiaschineseheritage.com/2017/06/the-bay-area.html.

Mechanics' Institute, "History of the Chess Room." https://www.milibrary.org/chess-room-history.

———. "Who We Are." https://www.milibrary.org/about.

———. "Mechanics' Institute History." https://www.milibrary.org/about/history.

———. "Mechanics' Institute Library." https://www.milibrary.org.

National Archives "1940 Census." https://1940census.archives.gov.

———. "1930 Federal Population Census." Last reviewed September 26, 2016. https://www.archives.gov/research/census/1930.

Nelson, Katie. "Clothes make the woman: 100 years of Chinese women and what they wore." *Shanghaiist*, May 5, 2018. https://shanghaiist.com/2015/12/11/a_century_in_chinese_wom-ens_fashion/.

"New San Francisco Emergency Edition." Special issue, *Sunset Magazine*, 17, no. 1 (May 1906).

O'Brien, Robert. "Riptides." *San Francisco Chronicle*, 1947.

"Our History." *Union Street*. https://www.unionstreetsf.com/our-history.

P. W. "Influences on Western fashion: The Chinese Effect." *The Economist*, May 12, 2015. https://www.economist.com/prospe-ro/2015/05/12/the-chinese-effect.

Parker, Frank. *Anatomy of the San Francisco Cable Car*. Stanford University: J. L. Delkin, 1946.

Pellissier, Hank. "Local Intelligence: Sun Yat-sen Statue." *New York Times*, June 12, 2010. https://www.nytimes.

com/2010/06/13/us/13bcintel.html?mtrref=www.google.
com&assetType=REGIWALL.

Peterson, Carol and Peter Uzelac. "The First California Theaters." *Trips Into History* (blog). January 1, 2013. https://tripsintohistory.com/2013/01/01/the-first-california-theaters/.

Polk, R. L., ed. *Polk's Crocker-Langley San Francisco City Directory*. San Francisco: R. L. Polk and Co., 1937. https://archive.org/details/polkscrockerlang1937dire.

"Port History." *City and County of San Francisco*, Port of San Francisco. https://sfport.com/port-history.

Rathmell, George. "Our Story." Tadich Grill website. June 2010. http://www.tadichgrill.com/history.php.

Robinson, Alfred. *Life in California: A Description of the Country and the Missionary Establishments; A Historical Account of the Origin, Customs and Traditions of the Indians of Alta-California*. New York: Wiley & Putnam, 1846.

San Francisco Theaters (blog), "Diana Hall." July 6, 2017. http://sanfranciscotheatres.blogspot.com/2017/07/diana-hall.html.
———. "Hippodrome 555 Pacific." July 7, 2017. https://sanfranciscotheatres.blogspot.com/2017/07/hippodrome-555-pacific.html.
———. "Hippodrome 560 Pacific." July 7, 2017. https://sanfranciscotheatres.blogspot.com/2017/07/hippodrome-560-pacific.html.
———. "The Thalia Theatre." July 6, 2017. https://sanfranciscotheatres.blogspot.com/2017/07/thalia-theatre.html.

Soulé, Frank, John H. Gihon, and James Nisbet. *The Annals of San Francisco, Containing a Summary of the History of the First Discovery, Settlement, Progress and Present Condition of California, and a Complete History of All the Important Events Connected with its Great City: To Which are Added, Biographical Memoirs of Some Prominent Citizens*. D. Appleton and Company, 1855.

Tingfang, Wu. *America, Through the Spectacles of an Oriental Diplomat*. New York: Fredrick A Stokes Company, 1914.

The Virtual Museum of the City of San Francisco. "Appraisers' Building—1906 San Francisco Earthquake." http://www.sfmuseum.org/hist2/appraisers.html.
———. "Looting Claims Against the U.S. Army Following the 1906 Earthquake." http://www.sfmuseum.org/1906.2/wolfe.html.

Wong, Edmund S. *Growing Up in San Francisco's Chinatown: Boomer Memories from Noodle Rolls to Apple Pie*. The History Press, 2018.

Whitlock, Herbert P. and Martin L. Ehrmann. *The Story of Jade*. New York: Sheridan House, 1949.

Wierzbicki, Felix P. *California As It Is and As It May Be*. San Francisco: The Grabhorn Press, 1933.

Wilson, Carol Green. *Chinatown Quest: The Life Adventures of Donaldina Cameron*. Stanford University Press, 1931.

Wikipedia. "International Settlement (San Francisco)." Accessed September 4, 2019. https://en.wikipedia.org/w/index.php?title=International_Settlement_(San_Francisco)&oldid=906174543.
———. "South-pointing chariot." Accessed August 26, 2019. https://en.wikipedia.org/w/index.php?title=South-pointing_chariot&oldid=886285193.

PERIODICALS

Ballou's Pictorial Drawing-Room Companion (Boston, MA). September 15, 1855, cover; May 23, 1857, cover.

Daheim-Beilage zu 27 (1880), cover.

Frank Leslie's Illustrated Newspaper. June 28, 1856, p 40; September 13, 1856, p 212; September 27, 1857, p 265–268; January 16, 1858, p 108; May 22, 1858, p 393; April 15, 1876, p 97; October 9, 1875, p 69; January 1, 1876, p 12; July 13, 1878, p 317; May 19, 1884, opium illustration; November 3, 1888, cover.

Frank Leslie's Illustrated Newspaper (German bound edition). 1850, p 61–65, 422; June 1850, p 115–117; October 23, 1858, cover page; February 11, 1860, p 407; March 21, 1874, p 205; December 11, 1875, p 480; September 25, 1880, p 259; July 28, 1883, p 84; November 12, 1886, p 732; 1890, p 356.

Gleason's Pictorial Drawing-Room Companion (Boston, MA). June 16, 1851, p 165; March 17, 1852, p 204.

The Golden Era (San Francisco, CA). 1860–1867.

The Graphic. February 23, 1878, p 204.

Harper's Illustrated (bound editions). 1856, p 616; 1879, p 292; 1882, p 291–292; 1881, p 377; 1883, p 567–569, p 732; 1884, p 196–197.

Harper's Weekly Journal of Illustration. November 18, 1865, p 729; September 12, 1868, p 581; September 18, 1869, cover; March 7, 1874, p 212; January 26, 1878, p 68; April 27, 1878, p 337; October 5, 1878, p 796; January 25, 1879, p 77; October 16, 1880, p 664; September 24, 1881, p 645; October 8, 1881, p 684; December 31, 1881, p 900 (bound edition); February 13, 1886, p 100; vol. 34 no. 1761, 1890, p 732.

The Illustrated London News (London, England). June 27, 1846, p 412; October 19, 1850, p 304; July 5, 1851, p 15; November 15, 1851, pg 596; August 9, 1851, p 181; January 25, 1852, cover; February 16, 1856, p 189.

Im die Welt. October 15, 1881, p 84; September 9, 1882, p 5.

L'Illustration: journal universel. 1850, p 84–86.

New York Illustrated News (New York, NY). February 21, 1863, p 252.

The Northwest Illustrated Monthly Magazine 7, no. 12 (December 1889), cover.

Rao, Nancy Yunhwa. "The Public Face of Chinatown: Actresses, Actors, Playwrights, and Audiences of Chinatown Theaters in San Francisco during the 1920s." *Journal of the Society for American Music* 5, no. 2 (2011): 235–270.

San Francisco Call. 1856–1900, accessed online.

San Francisco Chronicle. 1865–1947, accessed online.

San Francisco Newsletter. August 25, 1888.

The Semaphore. 1957.

The Wasp. 1867–1897.

INTERVIEWS

Curator at the California Historical Society

Curator at the Zamorano Society

James Riggs, historian

John Mattos, illustrator

Karen Page, Sacramento State Librarian

Members of the Chinatown Rotary Club, Commodore Stockton Street, San Francisco, California

Members of the San Francisco Chinatown community

Peggy Lee, antiquities expert at the Enchanted House, San Francisco, California

William Stout, architect and publisher

OTHER

Bodie State Historic Park, Office of Historic Preservation, California Department of Parks and Recreation.

Bridgens/Bixby map of San Francisco (1854).

California Historical Society Library and Map Collection.

Cathcart, Kenneth. Personal notes. 1937–1946.

Cathcart, Kenneth. Personal photos. 1937–1947.

Chinese Exclusion Act map, 1884. New York: Coward-McCann, Inc., 1962 (reprint).

Chinese Hospital records. San Francisco, California.

Langley's Business Directory (1915, 1925, 1928).

Madam Lazarinne & Ladies. Mansion House Place business card. 730 Commercial Street, San Francisco, California.

Map of San Francisco's Chinatown (1853). New York: Coward-McCann, Inc., 1962.

Map of San Francisco's Chinatown. (1857). New York: Coward-McCann, Inc., 1962.

New California Theater playbill. October 12, 1869.

Pacific Telesis Company records. 1927–1947.

Punnett, John and Ernest Punnett. Map of Union Square. California Promotion Committee, 1907.

San Francisco City Archives. 1863–1880.

San Francisco city directories. 1920s–30s.

San Francisco Municipal Report (1851, 1874, 1884).

Smithsonian Institution Archives. 1848–1900s.

ACKNOWLEDGMENTS

I owe a debt of gratitude to David Plant for creating "one more book" for his amazing library. His passion for history and people has been the single greatest contributor to this work. A lifelong builder and collector, he has shown a generosity of spirit and commitment to stewardship to which we should all aspire.

To Marti Schein: my wife, life partner, and business partner—and as such, also a research critic, accountant, and coconspirator for any and all projects, from scanning to map replication to primary printer reconstruction technician. This particular acknowledgment could go on for a while; she is a partner in every sense, and one whom I can only aspire to be worthy of.

Thank you to the many neighbors, libraries, librarians, and community members who became resources for my queries and whose generosity of information and personal experiences helped direct my understanding of the map, including: Violet and George Wong; Peggy Lee; Gordon Chin; Howard Wong; Betty Fong; Ken Wu; Charles Gresham; Charles Fracchia; County Surveyor Bruce Storrs; Deb Hunt; Taryn Edwards; Diane Lai; the Mechanics' Institute Library; the California Historical Society and their staff and archive; San Francisco Public Library, sixth floor; City Archivist Susan Goldstein; American Chinese Historical Society and director emeritus Sue Lee; California State Library, Sacramento; Rotary Club of San Francisco Chinatown; the family of Sam Wo; the family of Doris Yee; the family of B.S. Fong; Ruth Low and daughter Elaine Chan-Scherer and family; Aubree Mladenovic, researcher extraordinaire, as well as organizer, compiler, and initial editor whose eighteen months of overtime as a staff member at Schein & Schein from 2016 to 2018 helped to create the original 450-page manuscript.

Thanks also to Kevin DeMattia and Emperor Norton's Boozeland, San Francisco, for their generous permission to use the scanned image of their 1878 Emperor Norton script #2513, a great rarity.

I would also like to thank Cameron Books, including Chris Gruener, Jan Hughes, Iain Morris, and the entire staff who worked very hard to create a book worthy of their audience.

And finally, special thanks to author-historian Lee Bruno, not only for his singular efforts to get all of the numerous previously mentioned people to intersect, resulting in the completion and manifestation of this book, but also for his personal efforts on my behalf, including weekly time for guidance, write-ups, and assistance with the necessary yet unfamiliar tasks required in the making of a good book.

RIGHT: A tray man carries his wares across a deserted street. In the background is the building housing the China War Relief Association of America, an organization dedicated to supporting China in the Second Sino-Japanese War. Prominent members included the Fong family, which enabled Cathcart to study Chinatown more closely than most outsiders (Cathcart, 1937).

FOLLOWING PAGE: This run-down building on Union Street is a remnant of San Francisco's early days, before it became a fashionable part of town. It originally connected the growing town with the more remote Presidio district, but became a prosperous part of the city during the Gold Rush (Cathcart, 1937).

JIM SCHEIN is the owner and operator of Schein & Schein Old Maps in North Beach, San Francisco, along with his wife, Marti Schein. With an archive of over 7,000 maps, 2,500 pieces of ephemera, and 4,000 books—including the Cathcart collection of maps and 3,500 photographs—the archives span the globe and all that comes with it. Schein, an expert on maps, speaks annually to the San Francisco Historical Society, California Map Society, California Land Surveyors Association, the Mechanics' Institute Library, San Francisco DPW Bureau of Street-Use and Mapping, and to private businesses around the Bay Area. For more information, visit scheinandschein.com.

COLOPHON

CAMERON + COMPANY
149 Kentucky Street, Suite 7, Petaluma, CA 94952
www.cameronbooks.com

Publisher: *Chris Gruener*
Creative Director & Designer: *Iain R. Morris*
Managing Editor: *Jan Hughes*
Copyeditors/Fact-checkers: *Lisa Ludwigsen* & *Laura Warner*
Proofreader: *Mason Harper*

Text © 2020 Jim Schein
Foreword © 2020 Gordon Chin
Photographs © Schein & Schein, unless otherwise noted below

Page 118 (top) © San Francisco History Center, San Francisco Public Library;
page 137 (bottom) © Western Neighborhoods Project, OpenSFHistory.org,
Emiliano Echeverria/Randolph Brandt Collection; page 144 (top) Courtesy
the Sonoma County Library

Library of Congress Cataloging-in-Publication Data available
ISBN: 978-1-944903-89-3 • 10 9 8 7 6 5 4 3 2 1
Printed and bound in China

CAMERON + COMPANY would first and
foremost like to thank Jim Schein for
entrusting us with his discovery of Ken
Cathcart's photographs and maps and his
fascinating exploration of San Francisco's
Chinatown through the icons of his
scrapbook map. This book would not
have been possible without David Plant
and Plant Construction Company LP, and
we thank them for their support in the
making of this book and for supporting San
Francisco history in general. We would also
like to thank Gordon Chin for his generous
foreword; Lee Bruno for bringing this book
to our attention and helping to make it
what it is; Iain R. Morris for his inspired
design; Jan Hughes for her editorial
direction and oversight; Lisa Ludwigsen
for copy editing; Mason Harper for photo
research and proofreading; and Laura
Warner for fact-checking, proofreading,
and copy editing.

OLD FERRY BLDG.

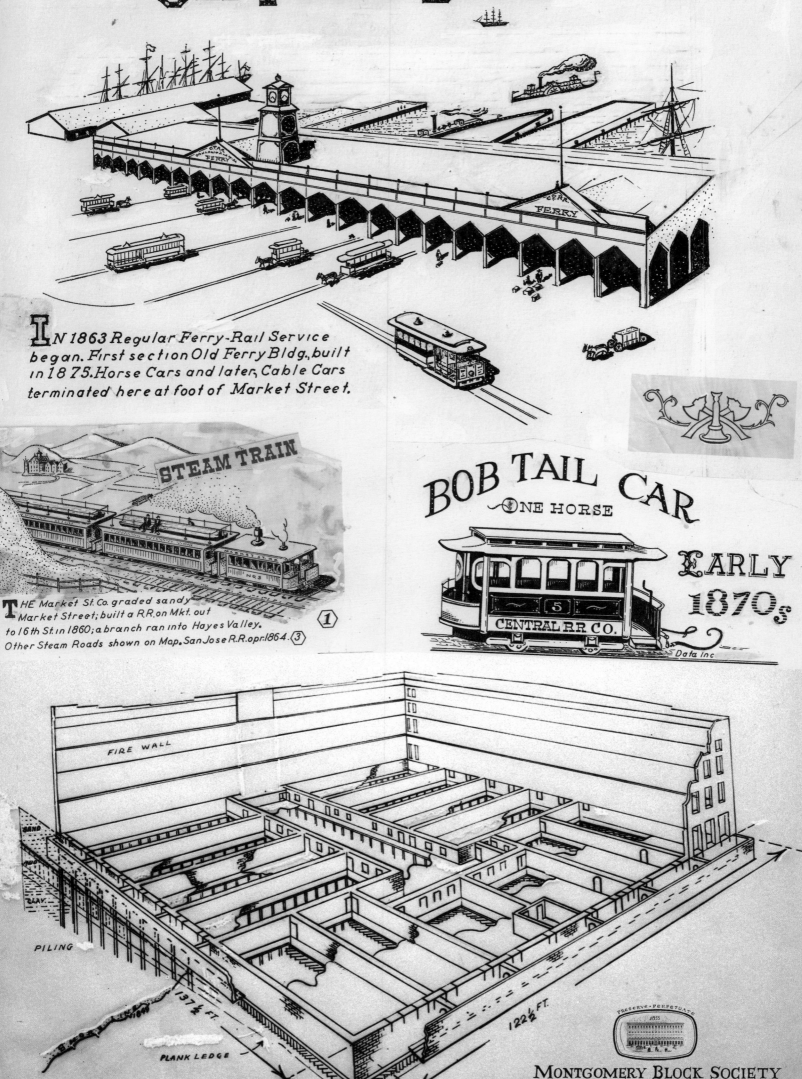

IN 1863 Regular Ferry-Rail Service began. First section Old Ferry Bldg., built in 1875. Horse Cars and later, Cable Cars terminated here at foot of Market Street.

STEAM TRAIN

THE Market St. Co. graded sandy Market Street; built a R.R. on Mkt. out to 16th St. in 1860; a branch ran into Hayes Valley. Other Steam Roads shown on Map. San Jose R.R. opr. 1864. ③ ①

BOB TAIL CAR
ONE HORSE
EARLY 1870s
CENTRAL R.R. CO.
5
Data Inc

FIRE WALL

SAND
PILING
137½ FT.
PLANK LEDGE
122½ FT.

MONTGOMERY BLOCK SOCIETY
FRIENDS ALUMNI